Capel Explored

Being an account of the history

of certain parts of the parish and

the memories of

its people

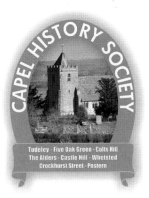

Published by Capel History Society

ISBN 978-0-9557134-0-8
British Library Cataloguing in Publication Data.
A catalogue record for this book is available from the British Library.

Editor: James Edwards
Design and typesetting: Paul Chalklin
Photography: Peter Tulloch ARPS DPAGB

Set in 11.5 on 12 point Times New Roman
Printed in Tonbridge by Complete Print Group

Published by Capel History Society.
Chairman: Mary Stinton, Secretary: Marie Smith,
Treasurer: Graham Wood, Members: Dr Tom Dalton, James Edwards,
Don Foreman, Gill Hoare, Bryan More, Jane More and Peter Tulloch.

Recycled
Supporting responsible use
of forest resources
FSC www.fsc.org Cert no. SGS-COC-003437
© 1996 Forest Stewardship Council
100%

Contents

This book is dedicated to all the men, women and children of Capel who have over the centuries tilled its fields, sown and harvested its crops, tended its orchards and hop gardens, coppiced its woods, shaped its landscape, worked in its shops and businesses, built its houses, learnt in its schools, worshipped in its churches, served its communities, belonged to its organisations, gone from here to fight for King and Country on land, sea and in the air and regarded this corner of our beautiful land as home.

Preface

There is no doubt that over the last twenty years public interest in the history of individual communities has grown remarkably quickly. One has only to look at the list of publications now available devoted to old photographs and historical studies of towns and villages.

At the same time there has been an explosion of interest in family history. This has encouraged researchers to look more closely at the social conditions of their ancestors, which in turn has given a major impetus to local studies.

In our own area of West Kent local history groups have published a large body of information which provides the kind of detail not available in more academic studies.

Local examples include "Beginnings and Bygones of Old Paddock Wood" by Jack Walker and "The Paddock Wood Patchwork" by the Paddock Wood History Research Group. There have been articles and books on East Peckham and of course Tonbridge and Royal Tunbridge Wells have both been well researched. This has left what I have often referred to as an historical black hole in the middle represented by Tudeley and Capel.

I have been told by a number of people that Tudeley and Capel have no history. This is clearly nonsense. We have two ancient churches, a large number of listed buildings, some of which date back to the landed families of the 16th Century and even further.

There were the iron workings of medieval times and more recently the parish was a centre of the hop industry.

It was against this background that a group of people came together in November 2003 and formed Capel History Society.

Capel Explored is the Society's first publication. It includes photographs of people and places in times past and aspects of the parish's history that will be unknown to many who live within its bounds. I am also sure it will be of interest to all those who want to know about the life of a country parish in this crowded south-east corner of England.

Mike Temple

Foreword

The first meeting of what became Capel History Society was held on November 11th 2003 by four local history enthusiasts. Mike Temple was one of them but after many years in the parish he was shortly to leave Kent for Lancashire. Like him they were all keenly aware of the lack of public knowledge of the history of our parish and wanted to do something about it.

This first meeting was conscious, of course, of those guides that did exist: Mike Temple's Capel Footpaths; the beautiful guide to The History of All Saints, Tudeley, by the late Mary Neervort Moore; Roy Tucker's account of St Thomas a Becket Church at Capel produced for The Churches Conservation Trust and Mary Stinton's The Hoppers' Hospital.

In addition to these four formal guides there was a survey undertaken in 1964 by Tonbridge School Historical Society entitled "Tudeley and Capel - Studies in a local community." This, however, was not generally available. It has, however, become a valuable snapshot of parish life in the mid-twentieth century. It tells of an era before the mechanisation of hop picking, heavy road traffic and the influence of substantial housing development in Five Oak Green. Some of the survey has found its way into Capel Explored and more will do so in the hoped for future publications.

The Society has more than doubled its membership and although this is its first publication it has mounted two exhibitions of historic photographs and documents at successive village shows and one at Capel Church. The Society has also established an archive of documents, interviews, maps and photographs that is being extended as research continues.

The Society wishes to express its gratitude to the many people who have shared, and continue to share, their fascinating memories, pictures and souvenirs with our researchers.

Mary Stinton

Mary Stinton

Chairman

The Parish

Don Foreman

What is now the ecclesiastical parish of Tudeley cum Capel with Five Oak Green was originally two, Tudeley and Capel, with a church in each, although from 1596 one priest served both. All Saints, Tudeley, was always the parish church, with Capel, as its name suggests, a chapel. Tudeley is without doubt the more ancient community, being mentioned in the Domesday Book of 1086, when it was known as Tivedele,

where there is a small rise, on which the church stands; here the soil is sand and stone, but in the rest of the parish it is a deep, miry clay, the hedge-rows broad, and filled with large and spreading oaks; which makes it exceedingly gloomy."

The two parishes developed in a particularly complicated way: for centuries Tudeley was in three parts, one either side of the parish of Capel, and another,

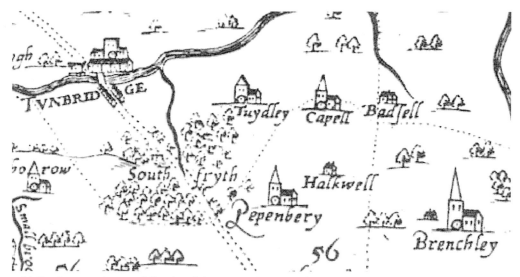

Phillip Symonson's map of Capel and the surrounding area drawn in the last years of the 16th century. Note the spelling of Pembury and the use of the 'f' shape for 's' in Badsell.

Saxon for 'ivy meadow' although some sources give the less felicitous meaning 'thieve's valley'.

Edward Hasted wrote in **The History and Topographical Survey of the County of Kent**, Volume 5, published in 1798:

"Capel is a very obscure and unfrequented place … the surface of it very low and flat, except in the middle of it,

'Middle Tudeley', in the centre of it. There was also a detached part of Capel known as 'The Hamlet', surrounded entirely by Pembury, roughly where Pippin's Farm is now. To add to the complication, the community of 'The Alders', around what is now called the Dovecote Inn, was in Pembury parish. This patchwork is well illustrated by the Tithe Map of 1843. It was not until 1885 that the two parishes were administratively united to form one widely scattered and sparsely inhabited civil parish, known as Capel. In 1934 parts of the parishes of Southborough, Pembury and Tonbridge Rural were added, and as recently as 1962 "At the Court of Buckingham Palace" the various separate parts of the ecclesiastical parish were formally united. But even in 2007 more remains to be done to achieve complete correspondence between the civil parish of Capel and the ecclesiastical parish of Tudeley cum Capel with Five Oak Green.

In 1801 the population of the parish was 731, by 1841 it had increased to 1159, and in 2001 it stood at approximately 2200.

It was not until the middle of the 19th century that Five Oak Green, where most of the shops and craftsmen were to be found, became the focus for settlement. Quite why this happened is a matter of conjecture, but perhaps it was prompted by the business generated by railway navvies being lodged there in the 1830s. This was evidently a period of transition in the parish: Five Oak Green does not merit a mention in Bagshaw's "Directory of the County of Kent" of 1847 in his entries for Tudeley and Capel, nor does it appear on Crutchley's map of c1850 (where the hamlet of Crockhurst Street does), but it is shown on the detailed Tithe Map of 1843. By the 1880s one third of the parish's population was centred on it, and since that time almost all new industry and housing has grown up in Five Oak Green. While it grew the original settlements of Tudeley and Capel were left relatively isolated, each standing in a green belt of fields with only farm buildings nearby.

Decline

But, unlike neighbouring Paddock Wood, Five Oak Green's commercial life declined towards the end of the 19th century, and by the Second World War the parish had ceased to be a self-supporting community. Gone, or very soon to go, were the wheelwrights, thatchers, blacksmiths, butcher, bakers, confectioner, drapers, shoemakers, tailor, builders and carpenters. It is hard now to believe that there were once five grocers in the parish, and we feel fortunate still to have the Post Office Stores on the green, although this, unlike its various predecessors, is more for convenience than for supplying everyday shopping as it would have been when a journey beyond the parish boundary was a rare event for most people. Only older residents will now remember the post offices cum general stores in Tudeley and at The Alders.

The churches

The parish is graced by not just one, but two ancient churches, All Saints, Tudeley, and St.Thomas a Becket, Capel. While both sit comfortably in the landscape the external appearance of neither is very striking, reflecting perhaps the modest communities they serve and the fact they have been much altered over the centuries. Nor can it be claimed that they have had especially eventful histories, the most significant thing to happen to either being the lightning strike to St.Thomas' tower in the "sudden and terrible tempest" of January 1639 which caused much of it, along with the south wall, to be rebuilt.

The glory of both churches is to be found in their interiors – the Chagall windows at All Saints and the 13th century wall paintings at St.Thomas's.

There are, of course, other church buildings in the parish, namely the United Church in Badsell Road, the old Congregational Chapel on Whetsted Road bridge, the former St.Luke's on the green, and the Hoppers' Hospital, which while not a church was run by clergy. It may come as a surprise to many to learn that the map of 1908 shows a 'Mission Room'

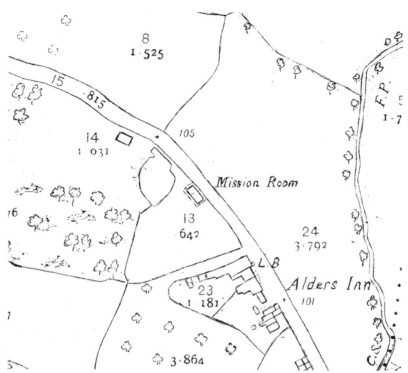

An Ordnance Survey map published around 1900 showing the site of the former Mission Room in Alders Road.
It stood about half way between The Alders Inn and the bungalow now called Chimneys.

in Alders Road, not far from the Dovecote Inn. Each of these played, or continues to play, a part in the history of the parish, and only the need to keep this overview brief precludes writing more about them.

Capel church was originally a chapel for pilgrims journeying from Chichester to St.Thomas a Becket's shrine at Canterbury, and no doubt there were houses of hospitality and victuallers nearby to serve them. The chapel was in the care of the Knights Hospitallers of St.John of Jerusalem, and their priest will have ministered to pilgrims and cared for the sick. Suppression of the Order, and later the dissolution of the monasteries by King Henry VIII, brought the procession of pilgrims to an end, and with it a source of income to the parish. The loss of custom, and the absence of parties of merry travellers, must have been keenly felt.

The iron industry certainly existed here in Roman times, and although to a much lesser extent than in such places as Lamberhurst continued long after they had gone. Kent in the Middle Ages was as much the foundry as the garden of England, but when more plentiful raw materials were discovered in the north in the 18th century the production of Kentish iron ceased, leaving Capel as a wholly rural backwater once more. All we have are the industry's pits and ponds to add interest to the landscape. It is possible, too, that the Black Death of 1348-49, which struck Kent especially severely, carried off many of the skilled iron-workers and caused smaller 'bloomeries' to fall into disuse. Plague evidently had a devastating effect on the area's population at large, but unlike some parts of the country there is no evidence of a 'lost village' in Capel parish.

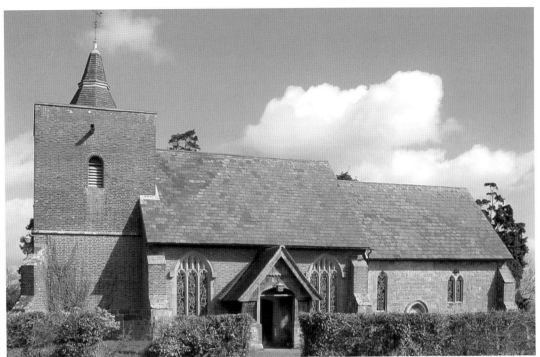

All Saints Church from the south before the installation of the porch door presented by the Teacher family in memory of Mrs Chloe Teacher's husband James, who died in 2003.

St Thomas' Church, Capel photographed from the south before the new East window was installed in 1905. The identify of the gentleman standing in the churchyard is not known.

In a 'Courier' article in 1968 the vicar the Rev Frank Forbes, said: "the Black Death which swept Europe ... infected the villagers, and the whole place – except the church – was burnt to the ground." He may have been right, but as far as can be ascertained nothing has come to light to support his assertion.

With the departure from Capel of the Badsells, the Fanes and then the Despencers, successive great landowners, by the early 1600s the parish's potential patron had gone, leaving it for almost 250 years without a resident squire. Nowhere

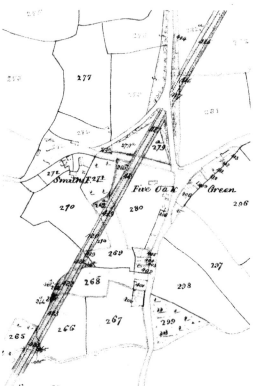

A section of the 1843 tithe map showing how the London to Ashford railway cut through the parish. It sliced through what is thought to be the original Green defined by a triangle of roads.

in Capel or Tudeley was there living anyone more important than a farmer. The d'Avigdor-Goldsmids did not take up

residence at Somerhill until 1849, and the house and park was not included within our parish boundary until 1934, by which time the squirearchy as a local force for good was on the wane. While it is true that they became valued benefactors, as the Goldsmid Hall and Chagall windows testify, they did not have the same sustained impact on their community, its landscape and architecture, as did the long-established Nevills at Eridge or the Pratts at Bayham, for example.

Building of the Tonbridge to Ashford line of the South Eastern Railway, opened in 1842, cut straight across the parish, and the 1843 Tithe Map suggests that the original 'green' of Five Oak Green, occupying a triangle of land roughly between and to the west of Moat Farm approach road and Whetsted Road, was destroyed in the process. It is difficult now to imagine the enormous upheaval this must have caused, not least because of the influx of scores of navvies who were billeted in Five Oak Green. But in the end, once construction was complete, the parish was not affected very much.

The railway station

Plans to site a station at Monckton's Arch, now carrying the A228 over the railway line close to Capel Grange, were thwarted when the landowner objected, and besides, the engineer, George Stephenson, wanted it nearer to the start of the Maidstone branch. And so it was built at, and initially named, Maidstone Road, and it was the tiny community of Paddock Wood which slowly but steadily grew as the century progressed, while the population and commercial activity of Five Oak Green changed comparatively little. How different things could have been! More recently, the Transfesa was also built at Paddock Wood, adding to the tendency for the vast majority of road traffic to pass through the parish, much

Crockhurst Street Farmhouse, formerly one of the many independent farms of the parish which are now private houses.

The attractive wall surrounding the d'Avigdor Goldsmid family burial ground in Hartlake Road which is listed as a construction of historic interest. Other walls in the parish are also listed.

to the annoyance and inconvenience of residents.

Vanishing farms

Farming has undergone a dramatic change, both in its structure and crops grown. Where once there were dozens of farms and smallholdings supporting, either directly or indirectly, almost the entire population, there are now but a handful of large enterprises. The majority of those houses named 'farm' or 'farmhouse', such as Crockhurst Street Farmhouse and Dislingbury Farmhouse were once independent agricultural holdings, each sustaining an almost invariably large family making its living from the land, as were some now less easily identifiable as farms, Half Moon Cottage, Stream Cottage and St.Norton's Cottages, for example. Yet more, notably Glebe Farm and the original Church Farm, Capel, both on the 1843 Tithe Map, have disappeared altogether. Very few Capel residents work on the land these days.

Within the lifetimes of many current residents the crops grown, and therefore the landscape, have changed markedly. Gone is the patchwork of mixed farming, many of the orchards and virtually all of the hop gardens, and with them the hundreds of hop-pickers who descended every autumn. Instead we increasingly see acres of rape, beans and linseed.

There were two isolation hospitals in the parish, one in the grounds of Dislingbury Farm and the other in Sychem Lane. Each served the wider community for something like 80 years, providing treatment for such contagious diseases as scarlet fever and diphtheria. Between them they could accommodate almost 100 patients. Both brought employment to the parish, and no doubt bought produce and services locally, but both had closed by the mid 1960s.

This view of Capel Church taken from Amhurst Bank Road illustrates a scene typifying much of the parish.

Something like one in twelve of our inhabited buildings are Listed, so are many other architectural features, making Capel's built environment particularly interesting. These range from the grand Somerhill, through two mediaeval churches, former Kentish hall houses, weather-boarded and tile-hung cottages and converted oast houses to humble agricultural buildings, tombstones and even walls.

And so to draw together the threads of this individual view of the history and heritage of our parish.

It could be argued that Hasted's "unfrequented place" has remained so because fate conspired to deny it large scale development: the iron industry collapsed, pilgrimages ceased, agriculture is no longer a major employer, the S.E.Railway built its station just beyond the parish border, for a long time there was no philanthropic or entrepreneurial resident landowner, the hospitals closed and greater mobility helped shut down local businesses.

A study conducted in 1964 described our parish as having "villages, still relatively unspoilt, havens of quiet, and one of the more purely agricultural communities of West Kent: they have, to the modern eye, quite considerable charm."

Forty years later perhaps we should still rejoice in the fact that history has in fact been kind to us, and that we live in a beautiful area, dotted with fascinating and attractive buildings, and, despite the ever-increasing traffic on our roads, in comparative rural tranquillity.

Bagshaw's Directory

Don Foreman

In 1847 Samuel Bagshaw, of Philadelphia, Sheffield, published his Directory of Kent or, to give its full title –

History, Gazetteer, and Directory of the County of Kent, comprising a General Survey of the County, and the Sees of Canterbury and Rochester; with a variety of historical, statistical, topographical, commercial and agricultural information; shewing the situation, extent, and population of all the towns, parishes, chapelries, townships, villages, hamlets, and extra-parochial liberties, their manufactures and agricultural productions, the Lords of the Manors, and owners of the soil, their public institutions, charities, magistrates and public officers, and the Seats of the Nobility and Gentry. In two volumes, with a coloured sheet map of the county.

The price, to subscribers, was 10s. 6d. (53 pence) per volume. That doesn't sound like much now, but in 1847, when an annual wage could be as little as a few pounds, it was a considerable sum.

The two parishes then being separate entities, Bagshaw gives each its own entry, as follows.

Tudeley parish

Tudeley parish and small secluded village, situated at the north-east extremity of this curiously formed hundred, 2½ miles E. b S. from Tunbridge, extends into the Twyford Hundred, and contains 1,593 acres of land, of which about 140 acres are in hop cultivation. In 1841, the parish had 112 houses and 643 inhabitants: population in 1801, 417; in 1831, 575: rateable value, £1,411. The parish is intersected by the South Eastern Railway. The church, dedicated to All Saints, is a small building, chiefly of brick, of which the tower was rebuilt about eighty years ago. The living is a vicarage, with the vicarage of Caple annexed, valued in the King's books at £4 16s. 0½; now £388: in the patronage of the Baroness le Despencer, and incumbency

of the Rev Sir Francis Jarvis Stapleton, Bart. The vicarage is a good residence, a short distance from the church, with a garden and about eight acres of glebe. The rectorial tithes are commuted for £234 2s.; and the vicarial for £114 7s. 6d.

The appropriation and advowson of the church, in the year 1230, was given to the priory of Tunbridge, where it remained till the dissolution. In the 17th year of Henry VIII. he gave it to Cardinal Wolsey, for the endowment of his colleges, after whose disgrace it reverted to the Crown. Edward VI. granted the personage and advowson to Sir Walter Hendley, at the yearly rent of 6s. 3½d., to hold in capite by knight's service. The Fanes were eventually possessed of it, from whom it passed to the Baroness le Despencer, as also did the manor of Badsall, lying at the south-east extremity of the parish, which formerly gave name and residence to a family of that name.

Caple parish

Caple or Capel parish, extends into the Lowy of Tunbridge, with which it was formerly entered, but was in 1841 returned with the Washlingstone hundred. It is situated opposite to Hadlow, on the south side of the Medway, 4 miles S.E. from Tunbridge. The parish contains 1,568 acres of land, of which 120 are in hop cultivation, and 90 acres in woodland. The soil is mostly a miry clay, except towards the centre, where it is of a sandy nature. The parish in 1841 contained 102 houses, and 516 inhabitants; population in 1801, 314; in 1831, 399; rateable value, £1,833 15s. The church, dedicated to St. Thomas a Becket, on elevated ground, is a small edifice, the nave of which has been rebuilt, but the chancel is very ancient. It has a tower and short steeple, and has long been a chapel, annexed to the vicarage of Tudeley. The rectorial tithes are commuted for £229 8s., and the vicarial for £55. A National School has been built on the east side of the church yard.

The rectory of Caple, with the chapel, was anciently part of the possessions of the knight's hospitallers, and was in the jurisdiction of their preceptory of West

Peckham. John Fane, Earl of Westmoreland, died possessed of it in 1762, from whom it descended to the present owner, the Baroness le Despencer.

The manor of Hadlow, in Tunbridge Lowy, claims over that part of the parish within the Lowy. It is usually called Hadlow Caple.

Tatlingbury is a manor, long possessed by the Fanes, from whom it descended to the Baroness le Despencer.

The Directory also lists Tudeley and Capel's most prominent residents, farmers and tradesmen.

The importance of the church at that time is evident, as the lists are headed by the Rev R. Boys, curate, and John Brooke, parish clerk. Next comes William Carden, schoolmaster.

These are followed by the shopkeepers James Pack, Charles Peacock, and William Wickenden, each described as 'grocer and draper', which probably means that they ran general stores selling a variety of goods, while William Crowhurst and John Manser had shops the nature of whose business was not specified, and additionally there was a baker, John Moseley.

Surprisingly there were three shoemakers: George Potter, Alexander Fry and Richard Fowler, plus a shoe tip maker, John Pearson. Given that the combined population of the parishes during this period was only around 1200 souls, one wonders how four people engaged in the footwear trade found sufficient employment. Perhaps it was because of the hard wear that the boots and shoes must have received when almost everyone worked on the land, or maybe they sold the shoes they made in the surrounding parishes, or offered a peripatetic shoe repair service.

The George and Dragon Inn which lies between the villages of Tudeley and Five Oak Green has served the people of the area with ale, beer and latterly a much wider range of alcoholic beverages for several hundred years. The building itself dates from the early 1600s.

Other tradesmen were Charles Wells, a tailor, Michael Smithers, plumber & glazier, John Wheeler, corn miller, William Skinner, carpenter, Lawrence Mercer, wheelwright & blacksmith, and Jonathan Pearson, blacksmith.

The parishes supported six drinking establishments. Thomas Pearson, James Platt and Peter Young are shown as keeping beerhouses, and Henry Sanders was victualler at the Chequers. Adam Geering was victualler at the King's Head, and also operated as a blacksmith from the same premises, while John Fordham, landlord of the George and Dragon, had a butchery business as his side-line.

There are no fewer than fifteen farmers named, although it is likely these are only those with the largest farms, many smallholders not being deemed important enough to be included. Not all the farm names are given. The list is: Mary Ashby, Jane Harvey, John Fagg – Church Farm (Tudeley), William Lawrence – Jococks Farm, George Maplesden (who had holdings in both parishes), Leffroy Playfoot – Badsall Farm, William Wickham – Plog's Hall, Richard Buggs, Richard Children – Shernden Farm, James Cox, Thomas King, James Pound, Stephen & Maria Southon, John Wheeler, and William Henry Winton.

It is interesting to see two women heading the list, presumably widows who had continued to farm, perhaps with family help, following the death of their husbands. As no other wives have been named, it is possible that Stephen and Maria Southon were brother and sister.

Poll books help identify a few more

An aerial photograph of Tatlingbury Farm before the storage shed alongside the oasts was removed to make way for a car park and the building taken over by Berry Gardens.

The picturesque Moat Farm which at the time of Mr Bagshaw's Directory was occupied by Stephen Southon.

holdings occupied by the listed farmers – James Cox was at Ashes Farm, Stephen Southon at Moat Farm, and William Winton at Tatlingbury Farm.

Samuel Bagshaw's Directory was, as its title indicates, an enormous undertaking: it is quite understandable, therefore, that it might not be without the occasional inaccuracy. At first sight it could be thought that one such occurs in the Tudeley entry, for at the top of his list of prominent residents, Bagshaw gives the Rev R. Boys as parish curate in 1847, while the board displayed on the west wall of All Saints' shows him as holding that position from 1830-1832, in succession to the Hon. John Stapleton, 1827-1830. However, in his description of Tudeley Parish, Bagshaw names the Rev Sir Francis Jarvis Stapleton Bart. as the incumbent, and it is indeed his name which appears on the church board for the years 1832-1874. How is this inconsistency to be explained?

In fact it is relatively simple, for this is a situation which could have come straight from the pages of Trollope. As Bagshaw states, the patron of the living was Baroness le Despencer, and Sir Thomas Stapleton, 6th Baronet, succeeded to the ancient le Despencer title, dating back to 1264, through his great-grandmother. This being a title which by the arcane rules of inheritance can pass through the female line, his grand-daughter in due course succeeded to the le Despencer barony because her father, Sir Thomas' eldest son, predeceased him. Sir Thomas' second son, Rev the Hon. (Miles) John Stapleton was, thanks to his family's ability to promote him, made Rector of Mereworth and Vicar of Tudeley-cum-Capel, enjoying the benefits of both livings, including, most importantly, their

ALL SAINTS'
T·U·D·E·L·E·Y cum C·A·P·E·L

1252	John ····		1702	Edward Dering
1328	John ····		1715	Wilfred Pyemont
1349	John Englaten		1726	Stephen Cowper
····	Thomas atte Gate		1750	John Hedges
1390	John Rycheman		1787	John Loop
1397	Richard Tickhill		1801	Joseph Sanderson
1401	William Estcourt		1805	James Stapleton
····	John Aspewell		1805	Joseph Sanderson
1418	William Appleby		1818	William Salmon
····	John Sugglesthorne		1827	Hon John Stapleton
1425	John Filboyne		1830	Richard Boys
1426	Robert Horton		1832	Sir Francis Stapleton
····	John Pery		1874	William Hayman
1442	Arthur Webster		1889	Frederick Case
1447	John Wode		1894	George Lachlan
1462	Robert Godchill		1919	Thomas Mason
1478	Thomas Brown		1924	Harry Capel
····	Richard Person		1947	Oscar George
1515	Henry Smith		1961	Frank Forbes
1529	Edward Keet		1975	Francis Minay
1538	Hugh Owen		1982	Sidney Riley
1540	Thomas Starkey		1999	Jeremy Ive
1544	John Gaile			
1570	John Harris			
1596	Nicholas Pownall			
1598	Robert Newman			
1624	Thomas Tharny			
1633	Edward Wallis			
1660	Samuel Vanderlure			
1700	Stephen Lyon			

CALLIGRAPHY · ANNA ROWLEY · 2001

The board on the south-west wall of All Saints Church showing the names of the incumbents from 1252.
For the first 145 years of the record four of the five listed were named John.

income. Unfortunately he died in 1830, aged only 29, after just three years in office. It is reasonable to speculate that this prompted a search for another family member to take his place and be the third Stapleton in 25 years (James Stapleton was briefly Vicar of Tudeley in 1805) to receive the parish tithes. During the interregnum the Rev Richard Boys was entrusted with (or asked to continue) the spiritual care of Tudeley and Capel's people, and resided in the vicarage. Given the fact that his niece was by now Baroness le Despencer and had the living in her gift, it can have come as no surprise when in 1832 the 25-year-old third son, Sir Francis Stapleton, who had succeeded his father as 7th Baronet, followed his elder brother as the incumbent of both Mereworth and Tudeley. He is quite properly recorded as such on the church board, but while content to receive the tithes had no intention of residing in such an out-of-the-way place and paid Richard Boys a lesser sum to carry on doing the job for him! Anyone who has read Trollope's book, The Warden, will

The generosity of the family of Baroness le Despencer and her husband Viscount Falmouth is remembered in the naming of Falmouth Place on the edge of Five Oak Green.

recognise this as a common and accepted custom in the Church of England at that time.

Baroness le Despencer married the 6th Viscount Falmouth, of Mereworth Castle, whose descendants inherited both titles, held a considerable amount of land in Capel, and gave plots in Five Oak Green to the community.

Capel Grange and the Holman Family

Mike Temple

Capel Grange is set well back from the Maidstone Road. It is a substantial building, one of the largest in the parish, and is now used as a residential home. The appearance of the house gives no clue as to its origins. In fact it dates to a period before 1640, a date pin-pointed by the width of the floor boards in the oldest part of the house. They are 12 inches or more wide and boards of that width were rarely used in house building after that date. Many of the cross beams and studs (uprights) are said to have been taken from old ships and some of them still have the nails driven into them centuries ago.

Its history over the past hundred years is associated particularly with the Rev Holman whose wife purchased the house in 1897. He subsequently contributed to the religious life of the community for many years. His origins and early life are not widely known, but recent work has revealed some information although there remain uncertainties about some aspects of his career.

The Holman Family

A tablet in the United Church at Five Oak Green tells us that Warwick Ryder Holman was born on 4th September 1862 whilst an obituary in the URC yearbook for 1946 tells us that his place of birth was at Lee Mill, a small community about two miles to the west of Ivybridge in Devon. His family owned a paper mill there, and a history of Lee Mill Independent Church published in May 1883 describes the close involvement of the Holman family with the beginnings and growth of that church.

Benjamin Holman gave a piece of

The Reverend Warwick Holman

Lee Mill for at least a year. During the four years after 1883, he trained for the ministry at Cheshunt College and following this gained experience at the Congregational Church at Angel Road, Worcester. He remained there without any particular responsibility until he accepted the pastorate at St Stephen's, Rochdale, a post he held from 1887 to 1892. It is not known how Warwick Holman was employed in the following five years, but his wife purchased Capel Grange Farm on 3rd April 1897. What prompted this move to Five Oak Green is something of a mystery, as was his financial status since documents relating to purchase and later land gifts and disposals were invariably in Mrs Holman's name. As far as the church was concerned, he was listed as being retired in 1900, even though he was only

land and stone for the building whilst 'Mr Horton drew the lime; Mr Barons gave the sand and carted it to the chapel site; and Mr William Holman hauled the stone from the quarry'. The chapel was completed in 1835 when a Sunday School was formed by William Holman. A later reference records the gift of a new harmonium by Messrs F. and H. Holman. The first reference to Warwick Holman describes how, in 1882 when he would have been 20 years old, he held a Gospel Temperance Meeting 'when seventy blue ribbons were given to abstainers (and) twenty pledges taken'. This led to the formation of a Temperance Society in January 1883 with Mr B. Holman as sec-retary and Mrs H. Holman as treasurer. The church treasurer at that time was Mr Francis H. Holman and the 'harmoniu-mist', Miss Maud Holman. The family was therefore deeply committed to the spiritual life of their community from the perspective of the Independent Church at Lee Mill. The mill itself was unfortunate-ly burnt down in 1911 and never rebuilt, although the chimney still stands.

Warwick Ryder Holman married Edith Wright of Wandsworth Common on 31st December, 1882 so the couple lived at

An inglenook fireplace typical of the period in which the oldest part of Capel Grange was built.

38 years old. So there is a presumption that either any share of the family wealth originating from the paper business was managed by Mrs Holman and used to pur-chase Capel Grange, or that Mrs Holman herself possessed independent means.

Mrs Edith Holman purchased Capel Grange (formerly known as "Fobles")

The United Church of which the Holman family were such an important part.

comprising the house and land to the extent of just over 50 acres from the three owners, Robert Monkton of Lee in Kent, Robert de Bray Hassel and Reginald Edward Hassel, both of whom were residents. It was sold for £7,250 on 23rd April 1897 and records show that the vendors arranged a mortgage with Edith of £4,700.

The Holmans in Five Oak Green

Having settled at Capel Grange, the Rev Holman quickly became involved with the local Congregational Church that was then located next to the railway bridge in the Whetsted Road. The church was well supported at that time, and the building became inadequate for its needs. Lord Falmouth, who was then the major landowner, offered a site for a

new church, but unfortunately, there were legal difficulties with the Congregational Deacons at Tunbridge Wells under whom the local church was administered. A solution was provided by Edith Holman who offered a gift of land for the building of the new church under a Memorandum of Indenture dated 9th May 1908, an act that mirrored that of the family back at Lee Mill. The foundation stone was laid by Mrs Holman on June 10th 1908, the church being opened in 1910. Today, this is the United Church on Badsell Road in Five Oak Green. Further land was donated by Mrs Holman in July 1932 for the present playing fields adjoining the Village Hall. This act of generosity is recorded on two engraved stones that were originally placed in pillars on either side of the gated entrance to the field. It was later dismantled to cater for wider vehicles.

The Rev Holman, who by this time had become affectionately known as 'Bushy' Holman, then continued a long association with the church, the tablet in the United Church recording the fact that he was a Voluntary Superintendent for 41 years, having formally joined in 1899. At various times, he was also secretary, treasurer, auditor and choirmaster. He died on April 12th 1944, his ashes being placed in the wall of the United Church.

The Garden Cottage which for hundreds of years was home to some of the staff at the Grange.

Farming interests at Capel Grange were carried on by Frank Holman, one of their two sons. He married Dorothy Saunders whose father was the bailiff at Dunorlan Farm near Tunbridge Wells. Their only child, Hazel, married Cyril Waghorn, a labourer on the family farm, but this union was vigorously opposed by her parents. Although the couple lived in Capel Garden Cottage adjoining Capel Grange, there was little communication between the two families. However, it has to be said that when Frank later became ill with Parkinson's disease, his son-in-law did take good care of him and there was supposedly some reconciliation. Frank died in 1969 by which time Cyril Waghorn had left the marital home leaving Hazel to bring up their only child, Paul.

More misfortune

The family again experienced misfortune when Hazel suddenly died in the autumn of 1975 leaving Paul in the care of his grandmother. She in turn died only a few months later in early 1976. This meant that Paul, now in his late teens, was left to live in Capel Grange on his own. In 1980, he sold the house to Mrs Gillian Langstaff, who intended to turn it into a residential home, and he bought Badsell Mains. At some point, Paul changed his name by deed poll from Waghorn to Holman, a condition imposed by his

The rural setting of the house is best appreciated from the edge of the lake.

grandmother if he were to inherit from the estate, once more reflecting her unhappiness with her daughter's marriage.

One further disposal of assets was made by Dorothy Holman when she sold The Coach House to Stanley and Margaret Lyons of Chiddingstone on 21st November 1972. It was, however, in a desperate state of disrepair, and the property was sold two years later to Sydney King, a local builder, who rebuilt the Coach House virtually single-handed.

Mrs Gillian Langstaff, having bought Capel Grange, proceeded to convert the building to the special needs of a residential home. It was opened on 1st February 1981 with accommodation for 16 residents.

Exploring the upper part of the house in preparation for the changes which would have to be made to turn it into a residential home it was soon realised that there were Victorian additions which had probably been made without planning consent. Mrs Langstaff said: "There was evidence of two roofs at different angles allowing extra features to be added on. We obviously had to make several changes to the property, some against our personal feelings as it spoilt some of the beauty of the interior, but these changes had to be made for Fire Regulations to enable us to accommodate and care for elderly people".

The changes

Over the next ten years, extensive modifications and additions were carried out at Capel Grange so that, by the end of 1995, the Home was registered to accommodate 32 elderly people. One notable event occurred in 1995 when the house was connected to mains drainage, a rather important facility when so many are to be catered for. Extremes of weather caused problems such as the 1987 hurricane that caused extensive damage, and the droughts of 1988-9 when the nearby lake dried out and eventually revealed the existence of natural springs that fed it. This added to problems created by the 2000 floods when the lack of a dampproof course in the garden cottage was startlingly revealed.

Capel Grange continues to provide a sanctuary for many from the parish in their last years, a fitting role for this large house in its pleasant and tranquil setting.

A history of Capel School

Mary Stinton

Capel Board Schools in about 1910. Notice the unmade road, the girls in their aprons, the boys sitting on the gates at their entrance and one standing on the brick edge by the porch, for which he was likely to be caned!

Capel County Primary School was built in 1875 as part of the government initiative to standardise education by establishing schools run by local "Boards of Governors" throughout the land. The new school was called Capel Board Schools because it was designed as two distinct schools built on either side of a school house. On the left was the Boys' school and on the right, school rooms for Girls and Mixed Infants. Each would be headed by a 'Master' or 'Mistress'.

It was a fine brick building situated in the middle of the parish opposite the foot of Church Lane and Tatlingbury Farm. This central position was vitally important at a time when children walked to school from Tudeley, Five Oak Green, Whetsted, The Alders, Colts Hill, Crockhurst Street and from scattered houses, cottages and farms.

The attractive Bell Tower was needed to summon the pupils each day. The late Grace Dolding remembered hearing it as she trundled her iron hoop along the deserted road to school from Old School Cottages one-and-a-half miles away in Tudeley.

Capel National School

The new school replaced the old Capel National School adjacent to St Thomas a Becket Church in Church Lane. We do not yet know when this school was built, but it is clearly marked on an Ordnance Survey Map prepared in 1869 as "Capel National School (Boys and Girls)". Other clues to its existence remain, an oak tree on the grassy verge opposite Church Farm was, by tradition, planted as a memorial when the school was demolished some time after 1875.

The new church parking area, now known as The Glebe (meaning Church land), was always called "the old school playground" by the Buggs family at Church Farm across the lane.

The School Log Books

Fortunately we have tangible proof in the first of a complete set of seven well preserved log books spanning the period from 1873 to 1980. These strongly bound volumes contain regular entries by successive head teachers over a period of 133 years. Together with a full set of Admission Registers from 1869 to 1952 they are safely lodged in the County Archives at Maidstone.

The first log book entries by the Master, John Shorter, reflect his rather prosaic, matter of fact style:

March 3 1873 – Sent two boys home to have their heads cleaned.
March 7 1873 – Severely punished a boy for telling lies.

Many entries recall absenteeism, with excuses such as "no shoes", "bird scaring" and "minding the babies".

School was encouraged but was not compulsory until 1880 and free education was not introduced until 1891. A school fee of even a penny a week was hard to afford when families were large and the average wage of a farm labourer was six shillings a week. It seems that some relief was afforded to the most needy. However, the farmers encouraged parents to allow

their children to work in the fields at busy seasons and the extra cash was most welcome.

Census Returns of 1851

A hundred and eight children were entered as 'scholars' in 1851, 54 boys and 54 girls, but 125 boys and 93 girls were not, so it is clear that only one third of the children in the two parishes were being educated at this time.

Five teachers were mentioned, three locally born, Sarah Holmby aged 48, Jane Wheeler and Rebecca Scoons both aged 23 lived and no doubt taught in Capel at the National School. In the returns for Tudeley Rebecca Ware aged 21 from Coles Hill in Warwickshire is described as Governess of the local parish school and Amos Lipscombe aged 17 appears as School Master of Tudeley.

It is possible that there was a school in Tudeley. Certainly Old School Cottages and New School Cottages remain. Incidentally a beam in one is dated 1691. On a map of 1901 a school is clearly marked north west of All Saints Church adjacent to the Hartlake Road junction.

Capel National School was founded by The National Society, a philanthropic Church of England organisation. Visits by both Rev William Hayman and the School Inspector are regularly recorded.

In 1873 the Government Inspector severely criticised the poor conditions in this ill equipped school and commented: "I am glad to hear that new premises will be erected without delay. One serious defect, the want of sufficient desk room has materially affected examination results". As acceptable examination results determined the amount of the modest Government grant, this was a cause for concern.

In spite of the formation of a board made up of a clerk from Tonbridge, Mr W. Wickham, the Attendance Officer Mr Joseph Horton and five prominent citizens, the building of the Board Schools was delayed. In 1875 the inspector threatened to withdraw the grant completely unless the new building went forward speedily although he praised Mr Shorter's efforts under difficult circumstances.

Capel Board Schools established

By the end of the year the school was completed and Mr Shorter and his wife Suzanne moved into the spacious school house. His log book entry however was in his usual laconic style:

February 28th 1876 – Children took possession of their new school.

We detect a lack of enthusiasm, but poor Mr Shorter and Suzanne had to cope with 68 boys of mixed age and ability. By May it had risen to 101 and still no assistant had been appointed.

In May 1876 the Girls and Mixed Infants moved into their own department under the eagle eye of Miss Agnes Wheatley who wrote in her Log Book:

May 15th 1876 – took charge of school. Found children backward. Three classes formed.

She appears to have been a dynamic mistress who managed to attain assistance from the board and had high standards. She encouraged Mrs Goldsmid from Somerhill to visit and inspect needlework, giving prizes for fine sewing. Miss Wheatley recorded much criticism of girls and the pupil teachers whom she was expected to train. There was probably poor morale among her staff.

After a ten year battle for assistant staff

with the Board, the Shorters resigned in 1885 and Joseph Horton, once an attendance officer and now "Certificated Master 2nd Class with Parchment" took charge of the boys being paid £80 a year. Sadly he was found wanting and after complaints about excessive caning, poor attendance and abysmal results he left in 1888.

Family Teams

During the summer holidays a new system of Family Teams was devised by the Board to ensure sufficient staff at a reduced salary.

Mr Nehemiah Tink, Master First Class, Mrs Amelia Tink, Mistress First Class and their daughter Enid commenced their duties on October 8th 1888 on a joint salary of £120. Quite a bargain for such highly qualified staff. Attendance improved and at least 87 boys, 67 girls and 55 infants were being taught at this time. Unfortunately Mr Tink combined his duties with that of Attendance Officer and became very unpopular both with farmers and the parents.

A famous incident recorded in his log book demonstrates the antagonistic attitude of some parents.

March 1899 – A parent called at the school at 4.20pm and in the most abusive manner demanded to know why boys were unlawfully detained. As it was some minutes before school was to end I locked out Mr Swan by bolting the door.

He continued to describe how, when he let the boys out in order at 4.30pm, Mr Swan tried to remove his son before his turn. Rather unwisely, Mr Tink stood his ground.

Swan struck me in the mouth with his clenched fist and broke my glasses.

Mr Tink retaliated once and then:

Respectfully withdrew from the fray.

Although such violence rarely occurred, Mr Tink writes that he was continually faced with abuse.

This family team were very dedicated and skilled teachers, but without respect from the pupils and parents life must have become intolerable and in 1891 Mr John Clavey, his wife and two daughters were engaged by the Board

I might add that when I came to live in the school house more than 50 years later we were told by the caretaker that the ghost of Nehemiah Tink could be heard pacing back and forth in the attics. Although we never experienced this, it is interesting that an impression of his unhappiness and frustration had lingered down the generations.

The Claveys 1891-1904

This family team were talented and well liked. We have a record of a charming and well presented programme of Entertainment at Capel Boys' School for Wednesday April 20th 1898.

The Chairman for the entertainment was Mr E. F. Looker, a local shop keeper. Part 1 comprised 14 songs, duets and recitations featuring infants, girls and some staff. The second half was an Operetta, "Inspector for an Hour". The cast included Mr Twigg H.M. Inspector, Mr Fetcham the Attendance Officer, Johnny Stout – fat lazy schoolboy and a chorus of Dunces and Scholars.

We can imagine the wooden screens separating the classrooms folded back, desks removed and a stage constructed for the performance. A rare treat for scholars and parents!

The winters of 1894 and 1895 were bitterly cold. Ink froze in the ink wells and the old slates had to be used. Most of the pupils caught either scarlet fever, measels or whooping cough. Several times the school was closed and once had to be disinfected. Without inoculation and modern medicines these illness were killers. When Mrs Clavey, Mistress of the girls' school was absent for long periods, one of her daughters joined the team. However, in 1904, after 13 years of faithful service, they resigned.

Captain Hubert Johns 1904-1913

This is the first Master we can visualise for we have a photograph of him taken before 1913 standing tall and serious with spectacles and moustache. He wears tweedy knee breeches, long gaiters, a black coat with a high stiff white collar and narrow tie. Thirty six boys stare at us grimly with a teenage monitor equally expressionless by their side. They are warmly dressed and well shod.

Capt. Johns taught with his sister and his niece and did not occupy the school house where the new Mistress, Miss Webb now lived.

Mr John Large told me: "My dad was taught by Captain Johns, but he didn't think he was much good". However, the Board were obviously satisfied for he stayed for nine years.

Mr Charles Fiddis 1913-1948

This much respected Headmaster served Capel School with distinction for 34 years 4 months. An Irishman by birth, he was a big man in every sense, tall, active, sporty and a dedicated teacher. He really disliked official paper work and Mr Peters, his successor, said that he used a simplified filing system; a nail on the wall and a waste paper basket!

He was strict but fair, always ready to give extra tuition or write a helpful reference. He also instilled a love of wood-

The first picture of a master at Capel School. Capt. Johns, who arrived in 1904, pictured with the boys in the year he left, 1913. Many of them are wearing the traditional Eton collar and they appear well shod.

work, gardening and sport, his three great interests. He participated fully in village life as a Parish Councillor, a Special Constable, Village Football Coach and a regular Reader in church.

In 1938 Capel became a Junior and Infants School under one head and Mr Fiddis was asked to stay on until after the war. During this period two air raid shelters were built one of which is still in use as a store. A school kitchen was built onto the back of the old boys' school. Many graphic tales are told of friendly battles during wartime exercises between the Home Guard and the Army Cadets when the school facilities were used for training purposes.

His now elderly pupils speak of him with affection, though the discovery of

heaps of canes beneath the old school-room floor during later extensions in the 1970s seemed to indicate a strict attitude of 'spare the rod and spoil the child'.

When told of this discovery his ex pupils explained gleefully: "We used to put 'em down the knot holes when Charlie's back was turned".

A school stock book revealed that canes were ordered by the half gross (72).

"We deserved the stick," the old boys chuckled, "we were little devils".

A retirement tribute in the church magazine of 1948 speaks of the many parishioners who had been influenced by him: "No one knows them better than Mr Fiddis. He knows them and they know him, nor are they ever likely to forget him. His influence has always been for good". Mr Fiddis retired to Tonbridge and pursued his favourite hobby of carpentry.

Mr Roy Peters 1948-1952

Mr Peters came from a Kentish family of teachers. He spent four years at Capel before leaving to open the new Cage Green School in North Tonbridge. He was an able administrator and a sound teacher. His twin girls travelled each day into Tonbridge to primary school, eventually becoming teachers themselves. He died in 2005 aged 90.

Mr Barry Morgan 1952-1957

This head teacher stayed at Capel for five years. There were no major changes in this post war era, but again it became very difficult to recruit able staff in rural areas. Many male teachers lost their lives in the war and the One Year Emergency Training Scheme was only just beginning to fill the gap. Mr Morgan left to take up an urban headship in North Kent.

Mr Charles Kenneth Stinton 1957-1989

In 1957 a twenty-nine year-old Yorkshire man was short-listed for the headship which had been advertised nationally. He had trained at Leeds before his National Service during which he was commissioned as a naval schoolmaster. He first taught men and boys at naval training establishments in Portsmouth. In 1949 he was posted to the Far East as an Operations Room Officer and "Schoolie"

Mr Charles Fiddis, standing on the right, with the sports master Mr Cornish and the boys of the 1928 cricket team. Back row (left to right): Maurice Simmons, unidentified, Bill Jenner, Bill Sceal, Ted Smith. Middle row: unidentified, Alby Large, Ernie Phipps, Henry Young, Len Drury. Front row: Charlie Phipps and an unidentified boy

aboard H.M.S.Unicorn, an aircraft carrier serving with the UN Force in the Korean War.

A keen athlete, he enjoyed the many opportunities to play hockey, cricket, sail, shoot and take part in athletics on bases at home and abroad. He decided to sign up for a further short service engagement.

In 1952 he was posted to Devonport and married Mary, a school teacher from Oxford. He returned to civilian life teaching children in secondary and primary schools in Portsmouth.

He was called for interview as Headmaster at Capel on Whit Monday in 1957. The panel was chaired by Lady d'Avigdor Goldsmid. She was joined by Mr Harry Veall, Mr Bert Buggs and Mrs May Tolhurst from Bank Farm, Church Farm and Moat Farm respectively, Mr Sayward H.M.I. and Mr Eric Bryant Chief Education Officer. All of them became steadfast friends and great supporters of Capel School.

The Early Years

In December 1957 Kenneth Stinton, our five year-old son Christopher and I followed the removal van from Devon to the school house where we were welcomed by Mr Bert Humphrey, the able, industrious, witty and kindly caretaker. It was a dream come true!

Brought up in a rural area of West Yorkshire Mr Stinton had worked on farms as a boy and understood country ways. However, his naval experience had instilled a respect for order, efficiency and high expectations.

As we walked round the school it was clear that much could be done to make it a more comfortable and stimulating environment for both pupils and teachers.

There were open fires in the classrooms, lofty ceilings and inefficient radiators. New boilers and a false ceiling to conserve heat and provide storage space, created more warmth.

Outside toilets at the end of the playground often froze in winter, so oil lamps were installed when required.

There was no school field, so Mr Stinton and the managers badgered the Education Office and eventually land adjacent to the school was purchased, drained, cultivated and sown with grass. This field had been used to accommodate hop-pickers when we first arrived, but now the giant Brough Hop Picking Machine at Tatlingbury Farm had replaced most of these seasonal London workers. The end of an era!

Formerly the boys had to be walked to the village playing field each Friday for games lessons. Now their own field could be used for so much more.

Gradually talented and committed staff were recruited who did not disappear with alacrity at 3.30pm.

"Community Spirit – Country Style"

This was the headline in the Courier Newspaper in June 1964 when the school was featured in a three page spread. It provides a wonderful archive of images of children working in school at this time which is treasured today.

We were honoured when a group of visiting American educationalists were sent to observe the school in action and later the Head was invited to a reception at the House of Commons with them.

Mr Isaac Ellis the famous village wheelwright, whose grandsons attended the school, made us a fine Maypole.

(He had made the gun carriage wheels for the Royal Tournament and had been featured in a very early T.V. documentary.)

Mr Ellis with wheels he made for a gun carriage at the Royal Tournament in 1968. He also used to repair the gun carriage wheels for the Royal Horse Artillery.

Miss Relf, later to become Mrs Worsell, one of our most popular Infant teachers, wished to teach Maypole Dancing and formed a country dance club which became so popular that charming print skirts and yellow blouses were bought for the dancers.

Few children could swim so two classes were taken by Mr Stinton to Monson Baths in Tunbridge Wells at 3pm each Wednesday. They not only learned to swim, but were trained for Personal Survival Awards.

Choir, recorders, gardening and extra sport also took place after school, trained voluntarily by the whole teaching staff.

As years progressed film and slide projectors were provided, a kiln for clay work, two sewing machines and, much later, a BBC computer to enrich our studies.

A high spot of the year – The Gardeners' Show

In July sheep or cattle were moved from Tatlingbury field opposite the school and the caravans and trailers arrived. An exciting fair ground sprang up in preparation for The Gardeners' Show.

Children worked hard to prepare things for the show benches: sea grass stools, cane baskets, pottery and needlework were completed.

At 7am boys arrived at school to lift and prepare their vegetables and harvest flowers from their gardening plots ready for staging and judging in the show tent.

P.E. equipment was carried across the road for the sports programme. Races of every kind, skipping, egg and spoon, sack, wheelbarrow, three-legged and, a great favourite, slow-bicycle. High jump was often won by Brenda Veall.

There was rather keen competition from the fairground children, for there were money prizes, but all was controlled by Mr Stinton's whistle.

The May Festival

A favourite event was the crowning of the May Queen, seated on her flowery throne with her attendants on our new field, against the hedgerow thick with creamy May blossom. The children danced, the choir sang "Now is the month of Maying" and the old country airs were played on recorders. Games, stalls and feasting were soon in full swing.

The infants' Nativity play in 1965 before the school was renovated to provide a proper hall.

Uniform

A smart navy uniform with red, white and blue ties was introduced and a badge designed which united the parish. It was divided by the sword of truth and justice of the Crusading Knights who founded Capel Church. The helm, which at that time rested on the tomb in All Saints Tudeley, was on the left and the five oak leaves representing the village of Five Oak Green on the right. Above, the blue wavy symbol of the Medway which flows round the western and northern reaches of the parish was surmounted by CAPEL.

About this time pressure was put on Mr Stinton to apply for the headship of the new Woodlands School in Tonbridge, which he resisted; the Stinton family were now fully integrated into village life. Mr Stinton had joined the Parish Council becoming Chairman after Sir Harry d'Avigdor Goldsmid retired. He was a church warden and a committee member of the Gardeners' Society.

I now had five children, all of whom attended Capel School. When my youngest became five I returned to full time teaching as part of the school team. We felt sure that this parish was the very best place to work and bring up a family.

Modernisation

Dramatic changes took place in the late 1960s when Sunley Homes and Gough Cooper gained permission to build two attractive housing estates in Five Oak Green. The school role was expected to double and Mr Stinton was asked to work with the County Architect to plan the extensions required.

The school house was to be converted to provide an administrative centre. A broad light corridor was designed to link the fine Victorian buildings with a spacious hall/gymnasium flanked by four modern classrooms. At last the children would have indoor toilets and more spacious cloakrooms.

The west end became a designated dining room with a wide hatch opening to an airy, well equipped kitchen. Beautiful lined curtains provided blackout for film shows.

The complex work was well organised and, though it was noisy and intrusive, we never closed. The project was finished on time to everyone's satisfaction without compromising the Victorian frontage. We had a virtually new school!

The Centenary

In 1975 the school celebrated its centenary and a horse chestnut tree was planted to replace the one planted for Queen Victoria's Golden Jubilee, but which had been uprooted to make room for the hall. The children, parents and staff researched the school's foundation and development. Senior Citizens were questioned about the past and a photographic display was created. We have archived replies to the 45 questions that were asked. One reply was rather shocking.

"We used to climb behind the girls lavatories to push nettles through the cracks between the boards", chuckled one old gentleman. The modern children were aghast!

As part of our celebrations we formed a Parents' Association. The committee became splendid fund raisers and organisers of social events for children and parents alike. Our school dances with a full dance band were well attended and

Mr and Mrs Stinton with the Class One of 1971 – a class Mrs Stinton taught for many years. The photograph shows clearly the flat roof and walls of the brand new hall.

strengthened friendships.

Two parents, Mr and Mrs Goodman, who were architects, designed a reference library extension which was built after two years of fund raising. It was initially stocked with 700 books thanks to the help of parents, managers, sponsors and Kent County Council.

In 1982 a silver pear tree was planted with the help of every child to celebrate Mr Stinton's silver anniversary. A surprise party and generous gifts including four tickets for Glyndebourne acknowledged his work at the school.

Gradually, with new facilities, more instrumental studies were developed. Tuned and untuned percussion instruments, violins and a full consort of recorders were purchased and played enthusiastically. Musical Evenings were very popular with pupils and parents.

In 1985 the children were trained to use the new computer to store data during a national project organised by the BBC. They ranged over the whole parish collecting information, observing, measuring and recording. A talented teenage brother of Catherine Spoor, a computer student, was recruited as an advisor. It was exciting to access our work later at an exhibition in Hastings.

It was the following year 1986 that the Mammoth and Great Deer fossils mentioned in another article were brought into school by Mr Hobbs. Our subsequent visit to the Natural History Museum was a marvellous opportunity to come face to face with our earliest inhabitants from 20,000 years ago.

In 1989, a month before his retirement, Mr Stinton was honoured to be chosen to represent Primary Schools in West Kent at an Education Garden Party held at Buckingham Palace and hosted by Princess Anne. The Prime Minister and Minister of Education were present.

It seemed to be the culmination of his work for more than three decades with children and their parents at Capel School.

1989 to 2007

Capel School has welcomed five Head Teachers in the last 18 years: 1989 Mr Martin Garwood; 1993 Mrs Jenny Goody; 1998 Mrs Kerry Scripps; 2001 Mr David Smith. Each made changes and ran the school in their own particular style.

During the tenure of Mrs Janet Fletcher, the present head, who was appointed in 2004, much of the older building has been re-styled to provide extra office space and a fine new classroom has been built.

Recently the Parish Council provided a school flag to fly on the pole in front of the school. It is grand to see the old badge fluttering in the wind.

There are more historical pictures on the following pages.

The girls of Capel Board Schools and the mixed infants, only four of whom were boys.
It is thought the photograph was taken in 1915.

Mr Roy Peters who was headmaster from 1948-52 pictured in the playground with the school prefects,
possibly in his final year.

Mr and Mrs Stinton with their first two children, Christopher and Caroline on the lawn of the school house before they moved out to make way for more modernisation.

The school staff in 1989, Mr Stinton's final year as headmaster.
Back row (left to right): Mrs Shirley Turner (school secretary), Mrs Sandra Hatch (caretaker), Mrs Carol Stevens (domestic staff), Mrs Maureen Worsell (infant teacher), Mrs Shirley Fuller (teacher), Mrs Colleen Parrish (cook), Mrs Eileen Cavey (assistant cook).
Front row: Mrs Elizabeth Greenfield, Mrs Margaret Herbert, Mrs Mary Stinton, Mr Kenneth Stinton (headmaster), Mr Roger Lumley (deputy headmaster), Mrs Tricia Starr and Mrs Dorothy Chaffin, all teachers.

Mr Stinton taking one of the Wednesday swimming classes at the Monson Road swimming baths,
Tunbridge Wells, in 1964.

The boys at work in their garden alongside the school, also in 1964.
Both pictures were taken for a special article on the school by the Courier newspaper.

An aerial view of the school in 1963. It shows the horse chestnut tree planted for Queen Victoria's Silver Jubilee, an air raid shelter at either side of the school, the separate playgrounds for boys and girls, the outside toilets at the top of the picture alongside Mr Stinton's garage, the gardening plots and the nappies of the headmaster's children. The school is surrounded by an apple orchard since grubbed out.

Capel Schoolchildren Meet the Ice Age

Mary Stinton

A view of Ice Age Capel? This illustration by Peter Snowball is of a scene beside the River Lena in Siberia 10,000 years ago, but similar conditions and wildlife probably existed at that time in the Medway valley.

On January 31st 1986 the Tonbridge Courier carried a story which caused something of a stir in the parish, but the young pupils of Capel School knew all about it and had been eagerly waiting to see it in print.

The headline read "**Prehistory brought to the classroom**". The report was accompanied by a photograph of Daniel West holding a huge ridged mammoth tooth, Julie Lucas with a curved mammoth tusk and Fiona Avis holding the jawbone of a Megacerous Giganteus, the Great Irish Elk.

Julie was particularly proud because it was her Grandfather, Mr David Hobbs, a keen amateur historian and lorry driver for a gravel extraction company who, on a crisp October morning in 1985, had burst uncharacteristically into the classroom with amazing news.

In working clothes and muddy boots, his face jubilant, he approached my desk opening a large bag of dripping gravel encrusted artefacts.

"I've got some fossils for you Mrs Stinton" he announced gleefully, "the digger unearthed them in Whetsted and dumped them in my lorry. I think there's the jaw bone of a sabre-toothed tiger.

They're for you. I must get back".

In the main he was correct, although the jaw bone proved to be that of the largest deer ever to live upon this earth and extinct for nearly 10,000 years, the Great Irish Elk, Megacerous Giganteus.

Seven feet at the shoulder, this huge creature bore incredible antlers spanning twelve feet, and weighing 40 kg. These were shed and re-grown each year. The Elk's diet therefore required high levels of minerals such as calcium and phosphorus to maintain this massive growth. Grazing over moist grassland, eating mineral rich plants such as willow, it consumed up to 40 kg a day. Willows are still abundant on the river banks and in hedgerows in the Whetsted region of our parish today 10,000 years later!

The children learned, however, that modern research has shown that Megacerus Giganteus was neither Irish nor an elk. Great quantities of its antlers were found in Irish bogs throughout the centuries and indeed adorn the walls of many castles and hunting lodges in Ireland. But this great deer ranged throughout Europe, Northern Asia and North Africa during glacial periods in the last million years. A fine, complete fossilised skeleton is displayed in the Palaeontology Museum in Moscow.

Originally it was thought to be of the elk family because of its elk-like antlers, but it is now acknowledged to be a gigantic deer.

We must return to 1985 and our remarkable journey of discovery.

When Mr Hobbs returned to his work my class reluctantly filed into assembly, whilst I hastened to the office to ring the Natural History Museum for advice. The experts there explained that we should allow our fossils to dry out slowly, for they had not experienced air, warmth or daylight for thousands of years. We were impressed!

To their astonishment and joy, the children discovered that they themselves would be allowed to scrape off the gravel, very carefully, with a craft knife suitably blunted.

Enthralling

There followed the quietest, most industrious and intensely enthralling few days of my career. As each group completed their work in Maths or English satisfactorily they took their turn to gather round their fossils, gently scraping away with pride and awe.

Poems and stories were inspired by these ancient teeth and bones. Research was undertaken in school and the Public Library. They painted, modelled, interviewed each other, speculated and made presentations to other classes.

Each night we wrapped our fossils in damp sacking and went home to dream of great mammoths feeding in the Medway meadows.

When the last particle of gravel had been removed, they carefully painted each specimen with PVA mixed with water 1:10 as prescribed. They were placed to dry slowly on a cool shelf and we all wrote a letter to the museum enclosing drawings, paintings and stories. A witty and positive reply arrived swiftly and the kind invitation was accepted *(see letter on next page)*.

On November 14th a coach load of excited children accompanied by some parents and teachers and of course Mr David Hobbs, now in a smart suit and

British Museum (Natural History)
Cromwell Road London SW7 5BD

Telephone 01-589 6323 ext

Department of Palaeontology

	Your reference
Mrs M D Stinton	Our reference
Capel County Primary School	
Five Oak Green	Date 16 October 1985
TONBRIDGE	
Kent.	

Dear Mrs Stinton,

Thank you for your letter and the enclosures which your pupils have so
carefully composed.

I have read all the letters and looked at the pictures and it seems to me that
the jaw in Lucy's drawing must be either a deer or ox, probably the former, and
not a sabre-toothed tiger. This is puzzling on account of your butcher's
opinion that he had seen nothing like it. The mystery must surely be solved when
someone here sees the bone. You might want to prepare the children for this
outcome since their letters suggest that a deer would be less exciting than a
sabre tooth. A deer is not at all a worse animal and at least it has managed to
survive until the present day which is more than sabre tooths have done.

I noticed that both the poems were about killing the poor mammoths. In one of
Richmal Crompton's William stories a well intentioned adult tries to interest
boys and girls in attractive birds like titmice and robins but William's opinion
was that vultures were more interesting.

Mr Currant is the best informed person in this museum about Ice Age mammals. He
has just returned from some field work during which it didn't rain and his hosts
gave him good breakfasts so he readily agreed to extend his duties to talking to
your children in the public gallery on 14 November. And he is certainly
prepared to identify and comment on your fossils. You could also bring along the
seedpod which some of the children refer to.

I think the key to treating your fossils is to let them dry slowly. They have not
been in air or daylight for thousands of years and it is a drastic change of
environment for them.

I have passed all the letters and drawings to Mr Currant.   Could you leave a
telephone message nearer the 14th about your approximate time of arrival.

Yours   sincerely

A W Gentry

highly polished shoes, arrived at South Kensington.

In a spacious room near the laboratories our pristine fossils were examined by Mr Currant as the children sat round him on the carpet.

They were warmly congratulated on their careful "conservation" work and were told that from time to time similar fossils were excavated in the Thames Valley and estuary and from the northern reaches of Kentish rivers. They date from an interglacial period, in areas known as "Terrace deposits". However, they rarely found their way into schools – Mr Hobbs glowed!

It was explained that at the end of an ice age, melting glaciers caused water levels to rise. Sediment and loose material was carried swiftly downriver where "downward erosion" occurred. Gravel deposits indicate the action of fast flowing waters which would carry bones and other fossilised remains until they became buried.

Mr Currant told the children that our mammoth tusk was a common find, as these impressive creatures, having migrated across land bridges from Russia and Europe, would thrive in many habitats. Typically they grazed in meadow like locations eating grasses, sedges, herbs, mosses and parts of trees.

This has been confirmed by the analysis of the stomach contents of frozen mammoths such as Dima; a baby Woolly Mammoth found in frozen ground near the River Kirgilayak in Siberia in 1977. Dima, naturally frozen for 40,000 years, was judged to be about six months old. It was emaciated, lying on its side and

Fossil finds unearthed from Whetsted gravel workings in 1986 by Mr David Hobbs. Daniel West holds a mammoth molar, Julie Lucas (Mr Hobbs' grand-daughter) part of a mammoth tusk and Fiona Avis a section of the jaw bone of The Giant Irish Elk.

the skin was intact. Even traces of the gingery hair remained on the feet. It was a sensation when it was discovered and remains frozen in the Zoological Museum in St Petersburg.

The pupils listened entranced as they heard that old alluvial marsh deposits (such as Whetsted gravel workings) were rich hunting grounds for mammals of the Quaternary period. (Quaternary is a geological term for most of the ice age beginning 1.6 million years ago).

The Thames Valley is the richest source of finds in Britain. London, we were told, is built on innumerable fossil remains from many different climatic periods which are regularly unearthed during excavations for building work. Hippopotamuses, lions and cave bears have been found under Trafalgar Square! In 1938 fragments of the skull of a very early man were found at Swanscombe in Kent; not far from the Bluewater shopping centre.

This evidence and cave paintings of ice age creatures such as Woolly Mammoths, Great Deer and Woolly Rhinoceros found in France and Spain, dating back 14,000 years and beyond, suggest that our mammoth and giant elk might have been hunted by prehistoric Capel citizens. No hard evidence exists – yet.

We were given a guided tour of the Palaeontology galleries to view an impressive array of Ice Age creatures which had been reconstructed and displayed against their relevant habitats. Our fossils began

A painting of Megacerous Giganteus (The Great Irish Elk). The animal was distributed widely across Europe from 400,000 to 10,000 years ago. It stood two metres high at the shoulder, its massive antlers weighed between 30 and 40 kg and were grown and shed annually.

Children from Class One and their teacher Mrs Mary Stinton pose with their fossil and Ice Age display.

to fit into the complex pattern of climate change, evolution and discovery.

Finally we were addressed by Anthony Sutcliffe, distinguished authority on the Quaternary period and a Mammalian Palaeontologist who fortuitously had that very month had his scholarly definitive book "On the track of Ice Age Mammals", published. We were presented with a signed copy for our school library.

He discussed the effects of climate change on the world in ancient times and today. Then he examined our fossils. It was explained that the depository of the museum, a huge warehouse, was full of such fossils as ours.

"Why not take them back to school and start your own museum", he suggested. It seemed a perfect plan.

A glass fronted cupboard in the rear entrance corridor was allocated and soon the display was complete, surrounded by a comprehensive display of the children's written work, illustrations and models for all to enjoy.

It was a unique opportunity for our pupils to glimpse the very earliest inhabitants of our parish, to experience the significance of archaeology and to follow through focussed research and contact with authoritative experts. Learning had become meaningful and fun!

Incidentally, the seed pod mentioned in Dr Gentry's letter had been found during gravel extraction near Ploggs Hall at Whetsted. It was the size and shape of a large Kiwi fruit. The weight and texture of the pod was that of a heavy, lightly scored and patterned stone. After pollen dating we heard from the museum that it had survived 1.5 million years from a period when this valley was full of tropical vegetation. As it was a new find it was retained by the museum.

Since my retirement in 1989 the fossils have disappeared. The present head at Capel Primary School has instituted a search, but they have not been found. However, Mr Sutcliffe's book remains in the school library and the photographic evidence and newspaper cuttings have been archived by Capel History Society and also stored on a CD Rom.

In his interview for the newspaper Mr Hobbs was asked why he had decided to pass on his "relics" to the school where his six children and three grandchildren received their Primary education. His reply was immediate: "I'd rather let them go there than stay in my shed. If you interest two or three children out of thirty you've done a good job."

A Century of Care in Capel

Jane More

The Sychem Lane hospital and its extensive grounds showing the distinctive Redwood tree. Behind the tree are the wards and at the bottom left, next to the entrance, the administration block.

The old adage "Two's company, three's a crowd" certainly did not apply to Capel during the first half of the 20th century when the parish contained three hospitals – the Hospital for Infectious Diseases in Sychem Lane, the Little Hoppers Hospital and the Smallpox Hospital in Dislingbury Lane, also known as Half Moon Lane.

Infectious Diseases

The hospital in Sychem Lane was built in 1887 and was known as The Tonbridge Rural District Infectious Diseases Hospital. Kelly's Directory records in 1924 that the hospital "can treat 70 inmates". An official form completed in 1934 states that the diseases treated were scarlet fever, enteric fever and diphtheria. There were then three hospital blocks accommodating 49 beds in six wards and three cubicles. At that time five nursing and seven domestic staff could be accommodated. The site covered three acres and, besides the wards, included a hand laundry, mortuary, administrative block situated near the entrance gates and a motor ambulance was kept at the hospital.

In 1948 the hospital could house 40-50 patients. Many of them, mainly children, who were treated at the hospital will remember their time there in isolation when suffering from scarlet fever and

diphtheria, a serious illness often result-
ing in death.

Confirmation of scarlet fever meant
being taken to Capel in an ancient brown
ambulance, successor to the horse-drawn
"fever cab" operated by the late Ted
Morley, Tonbridge's best-known cabman.
Once the patient had left for the hospital
their home was sealed and thoroughly
disinfected.

Scarlet fever patients spent six weeks
in Capel isolated from their families
who could visit but not approach. A
former patient recalls that even an uncle's
sympathetic sixpence had to be fumigated
before being handed on via a member of
staff. All one's clothing was taken away
and "baked" in a vast cylindrical oven.
The food – as remembered by a former
patient – was awful, consisting mainly of
white fish and semolina.

The hospital's location off Sychem
Lane fulfilled the requirement of isolation
from the outside world. Visitors arrived
by bus and in summer mothers desperate
to embrace their children were allowed to
see them in the garden but not approach
closer than five yards or so.

The hospital grew its own fruit and
vegetables, tended by gardeners who
were presumably immune to the diseases
treated.

During the 1960s the hospital became
an Old People's Home and memories of
working there were vividly recalled by
the late Les Large: "My wife, Bridget,
worked there for ten years and I worked
there for four years as an orderly. I
enjoyed it very much but the only thing
was that it got a bit too overriding. We
cared for these dear old people and were
liked very much by the next of kin who
used to visit.

"The Maidstone and District bus service
was very good; it brought the visitors up
there twice a week on Wednesdays and
Sundays. We also had the Toc H come
on Sunday mornings and supplied a few
sweets or tobacco, also the Sunday papers
to all those who could read. Mr Lundie
Rees from the Alders shop used to come
with his van with cakes, chocolate and
other things to sell. I also used to cut the
patients' hair on the three wards. It used
to be a forty-hour week for which you
were paid £10.00 and worked alternate
weekends but it was often 60 hours. We
also used to take some of the patients out
in our own time just to make life a little
bit easier for them.

*The Redwood tree is all that remains of the Isolation
Hospital and now sits at the centre of a group of
attractive houses.*

"Yes, we had a very good name, not only from the visitors, but from the doctors at that time.

"On my weekend off, I used to go to the Angel Football Club for their matches where the Sainsbury supermarket is now. After the match, I would go to the snack bar that used to be on the corner where the market is now. They used to sell hot drinks, sandwiches, hot rolls with different fillings, also nuts, fruit, shrimps, winkles and other fish foods. I would have my orders from the patients. Oh yes, they paid for them and I would go and take them on my bike. The patients really loved every other week so that I could get them their little bits of enjoyment. The list I had, had the prices on them. I would get the money from the Matron and she would get it from the patients.

"Capel hospital catered for thirty patients and was self-contained. What I mean is that it had its own laundry where excrement could be removed, then it was put into baskets to be taken to the Southborough Laundry for finishing off, and was returned weekly. It had its own Matron, Sisters and nurses accommodation plus cooking facilities. Also its own cesspool and boiler fired by coal and electricity".

The hospital later became an old people's home and closed during the late 60s. The near-derelict buildings stood rather forlornly boarded up for many years

Continued on page 61

The loggia in front of the Hoppers' Hospital built as a memorial to hoppers and those who worked with them killed in the First World War. The first donation of £1 was given in 1915 by the mother of one of those killed and the building, which provided shelter for social gatherings, was opened 10 years later.

Facing page: *The bright, vivid colour of the East Window which greets visitors to All Saints Church. Like all the windows in the church it is the work of the Russian born artist Marc Chagall and commemorates the death of Sarah Venetia d'Avigdor Goldsmid, elder daughter of Sir Henry and Lady Rosemary d'Avigdor Goldsmid of Somerhill. She died in 1963 at the age of 21 in a sailing accident off Rye.*

Page 54: *The Rolf Harris window in Goldsmid Hall. The artist designed it in the style of Marc Chagall as part of the BBC series "Rolf on Art" and it was decided to display it in the newly extended and refurbished Hall. It was unveiled there by Rolf on 30th May 2003.*

Page 55: *The mural painted by Estelle d'Avigdor and George Nathan in 1899, two years after the hall was opened. It shows the deterioration and damage that had occurred by the time the hall was taken over by the Goldsmid Hall Trust more than a century later.*

Centre pages: *A map of the parish showing how its border stretches from the edge of Tonbridge in the west to Paddock Wood in the east and from the River Medway in the north to Pembury Walks in the south.*

Page 58: *The new mural painted by the Tonbridge artist Cecile Boswell-Brown which retains the same rural scene with the same figures but interpreted in a modern, vibrant style. It was unveiled at an open day on the 3rd March 2007.*

Page 59: *Evidence of these wall paintings hidden under the plaster in St Thomas' Church, Capel, for hundreds of years was found in 1868. They were uncovered by Professor E.W. Tristram in 1927 and were conserved by Mrs Eve Baker and Mr John Dives in 1970. It is thought they were done in two stages, the first and lower section around 1200 or just before and the higher second section about 50 years later. As well as the north wall of the nave it is thought that at one time they also covered the south wall.*

Page 60: *The Royal Arms of King George II (1727–1760) in Capel Church. They were beautifully painted in 1739 on framed boards. They hang now on the west wall above the tower arch. Either side hangs the Lord's Prayer and the Apostles' Creed. The original position of the Arms would have been above the chancel arch; the Lord's Prayer and the Apostles' Creed on the east wall, above the altar.*

The Parish of Capel 2007

57

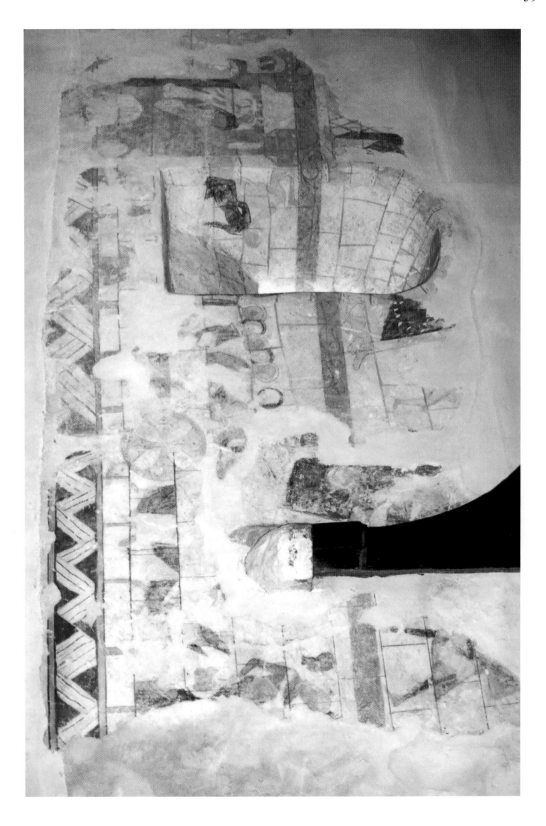

before their demolition in 1989 to make way for a small housing development – Redwood Park. The large and distinctive Redwood still remains however – a single reminder of the site's previous use.

The Little Hoppers Hospital

Hop production increased rapidly in the 17th and 18th centuries and by the beginning of the 19th century the extent of the harvest was beginning to exceed the labour available locally. By the 1870s with the total acreage approaching 70,000 acres it became necessary to import labour from a wider area and, with London only some 35 miles away, the prospect of earning some quick money over a few weeks proved irresistible to many who lived in the cramped conditions of London's East End.

On first arriving in Kent in the mid 19th century, labourers had to make their own way often by horse and cart and some on foot. On arrival they found only the most primitive accommodation was provided, farmers offering shelter in anything from cattle sheds to pig sties that were not even cleaned. The hoppers huts which remain in some places were not built until the end of the century. A combination of damp shelters, poor food, impure water and overcrowding inevitably led to poor health and outbreaks of disease. It was in an attempt to combat the results of such dire conditions that the Little Hoppers Hospital was founded. Probably the most well-known building in Five Oak Green, especially amongst former hop-pickers, the Hospital owes its origins to the late Father Richard Wilson, once Curate of St. Augustine's Church in Settles Street, Stepney in the East End of London.

In 1898 Father Wilson accompanied a group of his parishioners to Five Oak Green, to see for himself where they went on their annual 'holiday' hop-picking in

Father Wilson, founder of the Little Hoppers Hospital

Kent. He found that the conditions in the hop gardens were poor, especially the medical facilities, which were practically non-existent. This was brought home to him one evening when, walking back to Five Oak Green, he passed a woman who had walked to Tonbridge to find a doctor to tend her "sick" child. She told Father Wilson that the doctor had said the child was dead; her journey had been in vain. The young Curate of Stepney vowed that this sort of incident should never be allowed to happen again.

The following year he was able to rent a small end of terrace cottage opposite the village green. The rent was just 2/6d (12½p) per week. This cottage hospital opened mainly for the children of hoppers, hence the first 'Little' Hoppers Hospital. The cots and a small team of

The first of the Little Hoppers' hospitals next to the present day Post Office and stores on the green at Five Oak Green. It is now known as Wigmore Cottage.

The second of the Little Hoppers' hospitals with the decorative signboard attached to the hanging tiles. It lies between the green and Sychem Lane and is better known now as Stream Cottage.

The former Rose and Crown Inn pictured after its conversion, hoppers crowding windows and benches and one young chap keen to show off his cricket bat. Painted on the tiles is a tribute to Father Wilson no longer visible.

nurses were busy in their first year when there was an epidemic of smallpox.

A couple of years later a larger cottage was rented providing a separate surgery, babies' ward and nurses' accommodation. In 1908 the Rose and Crown public house was refused a licence by the authorities who said that with two inns and an off-licence Five Oak Green did not require another outlet for the sale of alcohol. Father Wilson and his Mission seized the opportunity of renting the building and in 1910 it was used for its first full hop-picking season. The facilities inherited were basic. Lighting was provided by paraffin lamps and the poor sanitary arrangements included just one cold water pump supply.

In 1913 the Mission was able to buy the building outright and the Little Hoppers

Hospital had established itself a permanent home. The facilities improved over time and provided much needed hospital accommodation for almost 60 years.

A report published by the Medical Officer of Health in 1908 estimated that in 1907 there were 12,000 Home Pickers, 10,180 "Foreign Pickers" from London and the large towns in Kent on the banks of the Thames and the Medway and 4,298 Gypsies. It stated that "people who were partial invalids or suffering from phthisis (tuberculosis) visited friends in the hope that the open air life of hop-picking combined with residing for a time in a salubrious district may be beneficial to their state of health". The report went on to state that polluted well water supplied in the hop gardens caused illness. Several districts with the sanction of the Local Government Board made arrangements for the supply of diarrhoea mixture to the hop-pickers and notices to this effect were posted in the Maidstone Rural District.

In the Tonbridge Rural District eight cases of enteric fever at Hadlow were traced to a farm at which many London hop-pickers were engaged. A woman came down from London when ill, the local doctor instructed her to stay in bed but she did not and died of enteric fever. The well used by the "foreign" hop-pickers and home cottages had become polluted.

Small wonder that in the light of such reports the Little Hoppers Hospital became of such value to the visiting hop-pickers.

During the 1960s hop-picking machines were introduced and the traditional influx of hop-pickers in September gradually ceased and "The Hoppers" eventually became redundant. In 1981 after years of neglect and a serious fire the old building was restored and following further improvements in the 1990s "The Hoppers" is now owned by a charity called The Red House, Stepney and has become a splendid self-catering centre for parish and family groups from London. Father Wilson would surely be content that the links established over a century ago are continuing today.

Dislingbury Hospital

The site of the third hospital in the village lies way back up a laurel-lined drive in Half Moon Lane which leads to Kenward and ultimately to Pembury in an area known locally as "The Plants". As with the Sychem Lane Isolation Hospital, scarcely any records remain and few people know of the existence of the corrugated iron buildings which were erected after the First World War as an isolation hospital for smallpox victims.

From Kelly's Directories we learn that in 1924 it was being used for the treatment of smallpox cases and in 1927 the Medical Officer was Dr Frederick Thomas Churchill Linton and he was still Medical Officer in 1938.

In 1934 an official form giving information about isolation hospital accommodation states that "the hospital is formed of two blocks, with a garage, mortuary, cottage, laundry, discharge block and disinfecting block." The hospital and other buildings were constructed of corrugated iron. There were six wards with six beds in one block and ten in the second block. Three nursing and two domestic staff were employed. The buildings were heated by coal fires and laundry was hand washed. Patients were accepted from the rural districts of Maidstone, Cranbrook and Tenterden. In December 1934 it was estimated that there were 25 people living within a radius of a quarter of a mile of the hospital and a further 55 within a half mile radius.

In 1957 the hospital was administered by the District Hospital at Pembury

Children of the Allcorn family playing outside their cottage, formerly part of Dislingbury Hospital, in the mid-1960s.

A photograph of part of the former Dislingbury Hospital taken in 2004 from the same position as that in the 1960s on the previous page. It shows the full extent of what was the Allcorn's home.

Some of the last residents enjoying Christmas in the 1960s at the old people's home that had previously been the Sychem Lane hospital.

but isolation hospitals were no longer necessary and in the late 1950s Mr Frank Allcorn, a farmer, and his family moved into the cottage adjacent to the hospital buildings which had been empty for some time. The family lived and farmed there until 1970, using all the land and the redundant hospital buildings. Mr Allcorn's daughter, Sue remembers hearing that in about 1965 the Bomb Disposal Unit was called in to disarm two Second World War bombs which were discovered on their land during ploughing. She remembers too that bread was still delivered in the area by horse and cart twice a week in the 1970s by Mrs Tully from Five Oak Green.

During the 1950s, when a pupil at Kent College, I vividly remember walks down to the "Hospital Gates". Little did I know that 50 years later I would be walking up the drive of the former hospital to discover that all the corrugated iron buildings were still standing, albeit surrounded and invaded by undergrowth.

One final medical note: In 1952 the front room of No. 1 Rose Cottages overlooking the Green was used as a doctor's surgery. Nos. 1 and 2 Rose Cottages (now known as Carrot Cottage) were occupied by the Hope and Fuller families.

In 1967 Kelly's Directory informs us that "Dr J. A. McDonald MRCS, LRCP attends at The Little Hoppers Hospital on Tuesday, Thursday and Saturday at 11 am". Following some complaints about the suitability of the accommodation by new residents in the village the surgery at the Little Hoppers Hospital was closed. Nowadays we are fortunate that the Surgery at Paddock Wood organises a clinic at the Village Hall during the autumn when those over 70 years of age have an opportunity for various health checks and advice in a relaxed atmosphere. It is a far cry from the days when the village contained three hospitals, but an acknowledgement of just how our health service has improved the lives of the population over the last fifty years.

Postern Forge and the local iron industry

Tom Dalton

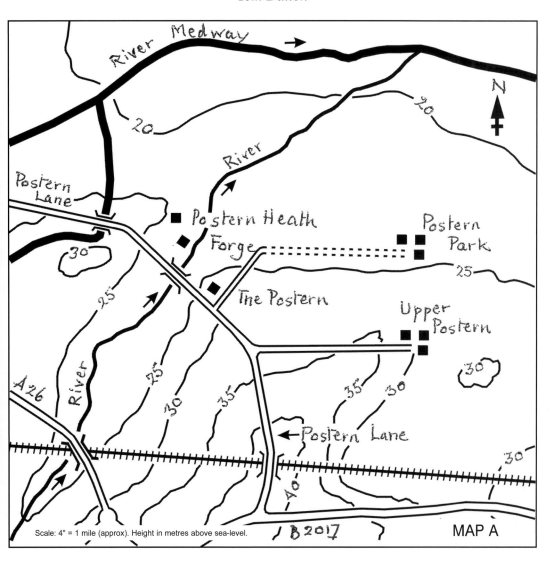

Scale: 4" = 1 mile (approx). Height in metres above sea-level.   B 2017   MAP A

The Postern Estate lies on the western side of Capel parish in an area of farms and woodland.

Among its orchards, meadows and arable fields are well established footpaths inviting walkers to enjoy its landscape. Pevenser in his book (1976) "The Buildings of England" refers to the Postern as:

"A charming and remote hamlet, though only a mile from Tonbridge. The handsome brick houses of the early 18th century make it memorable......"

The farmhouses of Postern Park, Postern Heath and Upper Postern were all built or rebuilt during this period as was the manorial house, The Postern (1757). The oldest domestic building in the Postern area, however, is Postern Forge. It can certainly be dated between 1553 and 1561 and may even be dated to the 1400's; The Department of the Environment's list of buildings of special architectural interest suggests 1480.

Its origin was industrial rather than agricultural. Postern Forge is the site of an iron forge, one of five furnaces or forges in what was then Tonbridge Parish (Map B). At the height of its productive life the forge at Postern contributed to an environment unrecognisable today. A local author, Frank Chapman, writing in 1976, commented:

"Tonbridge was part of the Black Country of England in Elizabethan times, when furnace flames lit the night sky and were visible up to 40 miles away when a great deal of smoke drifted across the land and the hills echoed to the pound-

ing crash of the trip hammers and while Tonbridge's own iron furnaces contributed to the dirt and noise, our small town suffered most from the incessant traffic of heavy wagons pulled by up to 20 oxen and sliding hub-deep through the mire on their way to London or the navy yards at Chatham."

Postern Forge lies to the north of Postern Lane adjacent to the river. The lane crosses the river valley on a steep embankment. This was, in effect, a barrier dam impounding a huge pond, essential for the water power used to drive the forge hammers. These were needed to refine and re-shape the pig iron "sows" into wrought iron slabs, cannon balls and a whole range of domestic products such as grave slabs, fire backs, pots and tools.

Dr C. Chalklin, in his 2004 publication on Iron Manufacture in Tonbridge parish

Postern Forge was formerly two properties. The door was the entrance to a cottage on the left. The main door is on the other side of the building and was the entrance to a cottage forming the right-hand half of the present building.

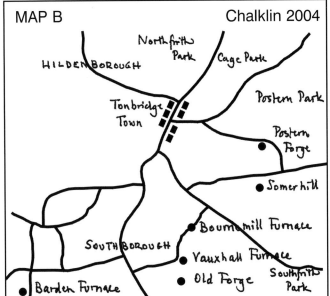

MAP B   Chalklin 2004

North frith Park
HILDENBOROUGH
Cage Park
Postern Park
Tonbridge Town
Postern Forge
Somer hill
Bournemill Furnace
SOUTHBOROUGH
Vauxhall Furnace
Old Forge
Southfrith Park
Barden Furnace

identifies five iron works in the vicinity: Postern Forge, Old Forge, Bournemill Furnace, Vauxhall Furnace and Barden Furnace as shown on Map B.

Local names such as Bourne Mill Farm at Ordnance Survey map reference TQ 5944 and Old Forge Farm (TQ 5942) still bear the imprint of those iron works of the first Elizabethan era.

Postern Forge depended for its pig iron upon a furnace at Riverhall near Wadhurst. The furnace consisted of a vertical tower filled with layers of small coal, charcoal and iron ore. The contents were set on fire and the molten iron tipped out into sand moulds forming "sows" (pig iron). A water wheel provided the power needed to drive the bellows.

The forge had a different role. At every forge or hammer there were at least two fires – the finery and the chafery. At the finery the "sow" was rolled into the fire and melted into a piece about ¾ cwt which was then broken off into a "loop". It was then beaten with a hammer which very gently forced out the cinder and dross to make a "bloom", a four-square mass about two feet long. There were then two or three heatings in the chafery to make the bars three feet long. Two men at the chafery could make up to five or six tons of wrought iron in a week. While none of this type of ironworks was listed in Kent before 1550, Frank Chapman suggests there was iron smelting and a bloomery in Tudeley in the 14th century. Any such early development would have been devastated by the Black Death in 1349/50 and 1363.

The Victoria History of the Counties of England (1932) confirms that there were important works at Tudeley during the whole of the reign of Edward III (1327-1377). As early as 1323 in Tonbridge Castle there were 26 pieces of unworked iron called 'blomysen' which were made into 423 bars of iron and sent to Porchester. Two years later 7,000 iron nails and 7,000 iron clenches suitable for shipbuilding were made at Tonbridge and sent to Porchester. In 1330 the Tudeley works turned out 194 blooms of iron and the next year 224 blooms of which 192 were sold for £16. At the Tudeley forge four blowers were employed, the master blower receiving 10s per annum and the others from 3s to 8s; they were allowed a farthing apiece weekly for drink! What appears to be the last record of these works is the entry stating the forge was not working in 1363, 'for lack of lessee and workmen on account of the second pestilence' (the Black Death).

New techniques for iron making were introduced in the early 16th century by French workers. The Wealden area offered many ideal sites with abundant forests for charcoal-burning, water power from fast flowing streams and easily accessible iron stone, often mined near the surface. There was a growing demand for bar iron from smiths in London and for armaments for naval warfare. By 1550 there were about 50 furnaces and forges in the Weald. By 1574, there were 51 furnaces alone but by 1664 a decline had set in.

Postern Forge had the three listed advantages in its siting – nearby charcoal sources, iron ore and accessible power from the river. Before looking at these in more detail it is important to note that an iron works was expensive to build and maintain. Capital investment was needed. Thus many of the iron making initiatives were taken by wealthy landowners. One such was John Dudley, the Lord of the Manor of Tonbridge, of which Postern was a part. As Earl of Northumberland, he was also regent for the young Edward VI (1547-1553). He signed a lease with Sir George Harper and Thomas Culpepper.

They were given the right to erect a forge on the Postern Lands and could take as much timber as was needed from John Dudley's land and as much ore as was needed from the Duke of Kent's estates. Harper and Culpepper then sub-leased the land to David Willard, a tenant ironmaster and it was he who built the Postern forge and associated cottages in January 1553.

Timber. A survey in 1521 described Postern Park as an area well-wooded with oaks and beeches containing 300 fallow deer. It was one of four paled deer parks in the area (see map B). In the early 16th century, forest covered most of the Wealden area. (The term "Weald" is derived from the Old English wald, for forest). To maintain a regular supply of charcoal the woodland needed to be carefully managed in a 12 to 15 year cycle. It has been suggested by Cleere & Crossley in their publication "The Iron Industry of the Weald" that a furnace needed about 2,500 acres and a forge about 1,500 acres of coppiced woodland. This was achieved by topping and lopping, leaving the heavy timber, especially oak, for ship construction. Between 1571 when clearance for farmland had hardly begun and 1664 (the decline of iron-making) three-quarters of the area had been converted into farms. By 1625 the Postern Estate or Park survey shows that the estate included 330 acres of arable land and 465 acres of meadow land, a total of 795 acres.

Iron ore. The Wealden area had easily accessible deposits of iron ore often dug from shallow pits. The chief source was nodules and tabular masses near the base of the Wadhurst Clay. Minor sources were also found in the Ashdown Sands and Lower Greensand. River gravels bound

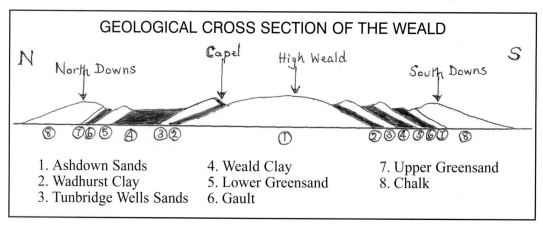

GEOLOGICAL CROSS SECTION OF THE WEALD

1. Ashdown Sands
2. Wadhurst Clay
3. Tunbridge Wells Sands
4. Weald Clay
5. Lower Greensand
6. Gault
7. Upper Greensand
8. Chalk

by iron cement were also used for smelting. Mr Gordon Sceal, a Tudeley resident, comments on the many shallow pits he knows of in the Tudeley woods, a clear relic of the iron mining. The Capel parish lies at the junction of geological strata containing iron ore deposits i.e. Wadhurst Clay and Tonbridge Wells Sands.

Transport for the ore, the pig iron and the wrought iron and finished products had to overcome problems. Postern Forge, for example, was supplied with pig iron "sows" by the Riverhall Furnace near Wadhurst, eight miles to the south. Such movement from Riverhall put great pressure on the roads and trackways. In 1573 the Secretary of State, Sir Francis Walsingham, reported on 'the great spoile and consumation of oke timber and other woods by means of iron mylles and furnaces and great decaie to the highwayes because they carry all winter time'. The deterioration to the road surface led to road repair levies on the foundry carts. By an Act in 1597 ironmasters were required to pay 3s for every three cart loads of coal or mineral and for every ton of iron carried one mile between 12 October and 1 May, for the repair of the road. For every 30 loads of coal or mineral and every 10 tons of iron carried in this period the ironmaster was required to lay one load of cinder, gravel, stone or chalk. For every load he omitted to carry and every rate he failed to pay, he became liable to a penalty of 10s. It is also recorded that several ironmasters were indicted at Lewes Quarter Sessions in 1600 for not laying down cinders during the summer period, including those carrying pig iron from Riverhall to the Postern forge.

Water. Winter conditions made overland transport of heavy goods across the Weald virtually impossible. Excess of water associated with iron making was a cause of complaint by local farmers if sluice gates were opened to release this excess which could cause flooding. In summer there was likely to be a loss of water for farmers, as water was diverted

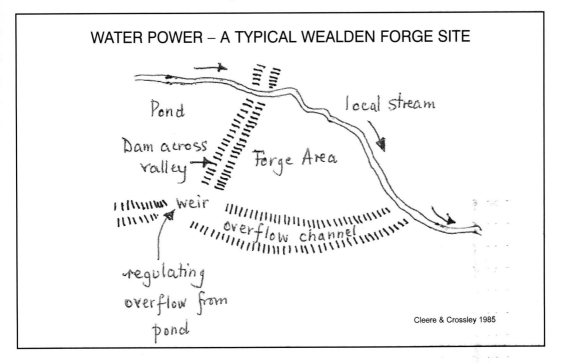

WATER POWER – A TYPICAL WEALDEN FORGE SITE

Cleere & Crossley 1985

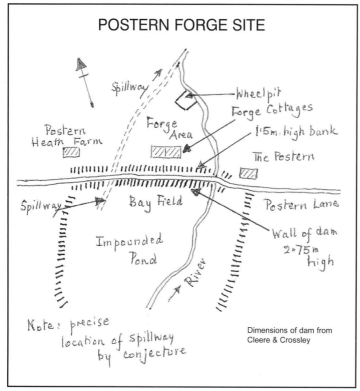

POSTERN FORGE SITE

Spillway

Wheelpit

Forge Cottages

Postern Heath Farm

Forge Area

1·5m. high bank

The Postern

Spillway

Bay Field

Postern Lane

Impounded Pond

Wall of dam 2·75m high

River

Note: precise location of spillway by conjecture

Dimensions of dam from Cleere & Crossley

and Cannon Bridge serve as a reminder of Postern's past? Postern's output of wrought iron products was most likely dispatched down the Medway to the Chatham Dockyards or by way of the Thames Estuary to the developing London Market.

Another local forge is identified at Rat's Castle (TQ594428). The bay is completely destroyed but the position may be identified by a hedge line to the west of an area containing heaps of forge cinders. The water system is now dry. This is possibly another of David Willards' forges. Most recent study suggests this may have been the site of medieval works, thus earlier than the 16th century.

into ponds behind the forge dams.

The furnaces and forges depended on well-harnessed water power in order to drive the water wheels which in turn enabled bellows and hammers to work effectively.

The 1838 Tithe Apportionment map calls the field south of Postern Lane where the water was impounded, Bay field and further south, Lower and Upper Pond Field, thus confirming the use of this industrial site.

The residents of Postern Forge have found a variety of metal fragments including cannon balls. Cannon would not have been manufactured here; a special furnace would be needed to accommodate such large objects.

However, could it be that Cannon Lane

By the 1650's and 1660's West Midland and Swedish bar iron was proving to be cheaper than that made in the Weald. The local iron works around Tonbridge were in decline as coal became the dominant fuel for smelting in such places as South Wales and the North East of England.

Postern Forge, once two workmen's cottages, remains the oldest inhabited building in the Postern. The impressive farmhouses and 'The Postern' house illustrate the way brick building replaced timber framed buildings in the 18th century as a result of the prosperity of Tonbridge following the opening of the Medway as far as the town, and the prevailing stable economic conditions. Nowadays these delightful buildings set in a somewhat remote part of the parish are reminders of the fascinating evolution of this part of Kent.

The author standing in what would have been the forge pond points upwards to Postern Lane running along the dam. It is 2.75 metres high on the upstream side of the river and 1.5 metres high on the downstream side.

The Postern, set in four acres of garden with additional orchards, was built in 1757 during the reign of George II. The front of the house nowadays is to the left.

The imposing front of Upper Postern Farmhouse now faces away from the road, which may suggest the original road or driveway has been re-routed.

The back of the farmhouse incorporates a front door and a magnificent catslide roof. It gives little indication of the grandeur seen nowadays from the lawn.

Charcoal burning

Don Foreman

Charcoal played an important part in the hop-growing process. It was the preferred fuel for use in oast houses to dry the hops, for not only does it give an intense heat twice that of wood, but has the added advantage of being virtually smoke-free and odourless. In addition, being lighter and less bulky than wood, charcoal is easier to transport – 10 tons of wood produce 2½ tons of charcoal.

The woods in and around Capel provided a source of both soft and hard woods, such as hazel, sweet chestnut, alder and oak, and as these trees are suitable for coppicing the supply was inexhaustible. Charcoal made from hard woods was best for fuelling the iron industry's bloomeries, while soft wood charcoal is ideal for hop-drying. Even old hop-poles, made of alder, which was in plentiful supply as indicated by the parish's main water

course being named the Alders Stream, could be re-cycled. Coppicing is still carried on in parish woodlands, and is the system whereby trees are cut off at ground level so that a dozen or even more shoots sprout up. These shoots are allowed to grow for five to fifteen years, depending on the size of wood required, and areas are harvested by rotation.

It is well known that in the Middle Ages the Weald's forests ('weald' is the Old English word for 'wood') were cleared for agriculture and to provide fuel for the iron foundries or 'bloomeries'. As the iron industry declined so, inevitably, did the demand for charcoal, but a study of relatively recent maps, such as the Tithe Map of 1843, gives a clear indication that at a time when hop-growing was increasing some open fields were re-planted with hazel and other trees which will coppice, and this can be no coincidence. One of

A woodcut of a charcoal burner at work in medieval times. The principle has not changed.

Capel championship tug o' war team in the mid-1930s, well known throughout the county. Back row, left to right: Mr Ryder (Manager), Maurice Wickens, Jim Hyland, Bill Mustill, Bill Passey, Roland Sceal, Jack Simmons, Tom Osbourne. Front Row: Jim Rideout, Don Taylor (the charcoal burner) and Isaac Ellis (Captain).

The Capel Football Club team for the season 1923 – 24. Back row (l to r): R. Wickens, the Rev Warwick Holman, W. Smith, D. Taylor (the charcoal burner), F. Langridge, R Walland, G.Avis, F. Looker, T. Jenner. Middle: C. Noakes, A Powley, C. Fiddis, (headmaster, Capel Schools), J Simmons, F. Powley, A Powley, T. Tolhurst. Sitting: A.Gilbert and P Simmons

these areas, along Half Moon Lane, is even known as 'The Plants', and James Buggs of Capel's Church Farm remembers his father showing him how it had previously been under plough.

The production of charcoal was an art practised by skilled burners, whose services were once much in great demand, for early industry needed it for the production of not just iron but also glass and gunpowder. During the eighteenth century coal took its place in industry, but coal was unsuitable for firing hop-drying kilns so the production of charcoal continued at several sites in this area, at least one of them continuing in use until the 1950s.

The Secret

The method seems simple enough, but the secret of constructing a successful fire was closely guarded, as the wood mustn't be allowed to burn completely and be reduced to a pile of useless ash. To make charcoal the burner would construct a triangular chimney of short sticks around which he would pile logs until the stack was about six feet (two metres) high. This was then covered with material such as bracken or straw, and over that was spread a layer of ash and earth, or turves, which kept out as much oxygen as possible. The fire was lit by dropping burning charcoal down the chimney, which was then sealed with earth.

To prevent the wood igniting and a major fire breaking out, which could ruin the entire clamp, it was vital that air should be excluded. That meant, of course, that the clamp had to be constantly watched, or at least checked every twenty minutes, and as the process takes up to five days this was a demanding task. At any sign of the crust cracking and fire breaking out the hole had to be quickly filled with turf or wet ash, leaving only carefully positioned vents to allow steam

and smoke to escape.

A change in the colour of the smoke from white to blue indicated that the burn was complete and the clamp could be allowed to cool for two or three days. Great care needed to be exercised when the clamp was broken open, and any smouldering charcoal doused with water to prevent it bursting into flame. Once the charcoal was cold it could be raked out, sieved, graded and bagged.

During the first half of the 20th century Capel had at least two charcoal burners, but the best known of them was a colourful character called Don Taylor. The Taylors lived at the far end of Whetsted Road on the edge of Five Oak Green in one of a square block of four cottages known to locals as 'Nippy (or Neppy) Square'. Don was a lively man, with a bouncy walk and a mischievous grin, as can be seen in the photographs, and was famous for enjoying a drink. Given his reputation it is not surprising that when he moved from the parish it was to become licensee of a pub, the Hop Pole Inn, in East Peckham.

Sportsman

Don was someone who threw himself heart and soul into village life. He played for Capel Football Club, and was in the Five Oak Green Tug o' War Team. In fact he was an all-round sportsman, as he was also an Army boxing champion. His strength was renowned, and his 'party trick' was to tie a handkerchief through the ring atop a half-hundredweight, grip the handkerchief in his teeth and then lift the weight!

Along with Isaac Ellis and George Twort, in 1932 Don Taylor was a founder member of the Capel British Legion Drum & Fife Band. Drawing on his experience as a former drummer in the East

Kent Regiment (the 'Buffs') he became the first Bandmaster.

Charcoal burning was a seasonal activity lasting a few weeks in spring, and Don would build his charcoal clamps at Tatlingbury, near the corner of Church Lane, and in a Church Farm field along Alders Road which was one of the parish's long-established burning sites. This field is still known as 'Coal Hearth', and has been for as long as anyone can remember; even now moles throw up black earth, the residue of centuries of burning, as they burrow through it. Before the method of building clamps was perfected charcoal was produced in pits covered in turf, so these areas of black soil can be very deep.

Labourers' wages

Charlie Simmons, whose family has long lived and worked in the parish, has in his possession a Tatlingbury Farm day book recording payments made to its labourers in which there are several references to 'Taylor' – no Christian names were used when referring to employees in those days. He first appears in the accounts on November 1st 1913 when he was paid 16/- (80 pence) for 'burning wood'. The next week he earned 18/- (90 pence) and the one after that a whole £1! He earned another £1 for the week ending November 22nd for 'burning charcoal', and the entry for November 29th records that he was paid the balance of £4 6s (£4.30) for 'burning 29½ cords of wood at 5/-' (25 pence).

The total amount paid in 1913 to all of Tatlingbury's 15-20 farm labourers, most of them working a six-day week, including picking and drying 473 pokes of hops, was £1,435.

As he was serving in the Army during the 1914-18 War Don Taylor's name does

not appear again until October 5th 1918, when he was paid £2 for charcoal. The balance of £4 5s 3d. (£4.27) was paid to him a week later.

The fact that he was back at work before the Armistice was declared on 11th November 1918 suggests that he had either suffered an injury or been sent home for a spell of well-earned leave. Whichever it was, he must have been heartily glad not to have to return to the trenches of Flanders.

Some charcoal burners would build themselves a shelter of logs, or a pole and canvas tent similar to a wigwam or bivouac, but on Church Farm Don Taylor had the use of a shed which can still be seen, although now in a very sorry state, almost opposite the farmyard entrance in Alders Road. Not only could he keep out of the rain, but even sleep there if necessary. During 'opening hours' it was far from uncommon for him to slope off to the George and Dragon or Alders Inn leav-

The charcoal burner's hut used by Don Taylor. He occasionally stayed there overnight to watch the burning clamp. It was also a retreat from the rain.

ing a young apprentice to look after the clamp, or rely on a passer-by seeing the fire break through and rushing to the pub to call him back to attend to it. A similar shed stood on his site at Tatlingbury.

So that he would not miss playing cricket for Capel on Saturday Don always built his clamps on Monday and timed the burning to finish on Friday. If any of his charcoal proved to be of poor quality, it was assumed he had rushed the job and that batch was described as his 'cricketing charcoal'!

It was much to Don's regret that none of his apprentices took to the demanding life of a charcoal burner, but local children loved to watch him building and firing his clamps, and he had no difficulty in attracting young 'assistants'. As a reward, Pam Jones remembers, he would give them a few of the explosive pellets used to split logs, and if they took them home and hid them in the domestic coal to frighten their parents when they went off, then that was all part of the fun.

So well known was he that The Kent and Sussex Courier of September 14th, 1951, carried an article about him.

FAMILY HAS BEEN 'BURNING' FOR OVER 600 YEARS

SIX HUNDRED years ago there was a Taylor burning charcoal – and there has been one in the Taylor family ever since.

Last survivor of this long line of craftsmen is Mr Donald Taylor, licensee of the Hop Pole Inn at East Peckham.

Mr Taylor says he and his family have been burning charcoal for 600 years according to records – and probably even longer than that.

When he dies the line will end, for he has no sons to take over and his brother will not do it. Mr Taylor is training a youth in the village, but doesn't know whether he will stay to it.

Mr Taylor told the "Courier" that he first started charcoal burning as soon as he could

walk. His father was an expert and passed on the craft.

He says it is an amazing thing that although he can burn the charcoal he does not know what actually changes the wood into charcoal.

Nowadays there is not the demand for charcoal that there used to be, and he only burns some when farming friends ask him to.

The work is hard, for once the fire is lit the burner has to stay with it for 72 hours. If the slightest thing goes wrong and the burner is not on hand, 15 to 20 pounds of charcoal can be spoiled.

During the war, when burners were very scarce, Mr Taylor used to stay by his fires for as long as three weeks.

He has tried the modern machines, but still considers the age-old way of burning is the best.

He makes the charcoal by burning on top of a charcoal fire. He piles the wood around the burning charcoal, covers it with grass and then with ashes. The ash is always raked back after the firing and in most farms the same ash has been used for hundreds of years.

Murder

One of Don Taylor's apprentice charcoal burners played a part in part in bringing a murderess to justice.

On 9th July 1940, Florence Ransom shot her lover's wife, Dorothy Fisher, her daughter, Freda Fisher, and their domestic servant, Charlotte Saunders. Mrs Ransom fled the scene of the crime, Crittenden, Matfield, and made her way with all haste to Tonbridge Station.

The whole story came out in detail in the report of committal proceedings which were published in The Tonbridge Free Press of August 16th, 1940:

William Smith, of 6 Alders Cottages, Five Oak Green, Paddock Wood, a charcoal burner, aged 14, said that on July 9 he cycled along the road past Crittenden towards Matfield at about 1.45 pm. On looking up the drive at Crittenden he noticed two bicycles. At about

3.20 he cycled past Crittenden when return-
ing from Matfield, and about 50 yards past
the house on the Tonbridge side he noticed a
lady's bicycle lying on the ground with one
of the handlebars caught in a gate.

Just before he reached Colts Hill he saw a
woman walking in the direction of Tonbridge.
She was wearing blue trousers, a brown coat,
brown shoes with crepe bottoms, and a blue
handkerchief over her head. She was carrying a brown paper parcel about a yard long
and four inches wide.

On July 15 at Tonbridge Police Station
witness picked out this woman at an iden-
tification parade. He identified her as the
prisoner.

Later at Alders Hill he saw the prisoner running in the direction of Tonbridge.

John William Elphick, of 3, Alders Cottages,
Five Oak Green, a labourer, who was talking
to William Smith at about 3.30-4.30 pm on
July 9 in Alders Village, gave corroborative
evidence of having seen prisoner during that
period.

William Edgar Playfoot, of The Alders, Five
Oak Green, a baker, said that while helping
with the loading of his van on the Matfield
to Tonbridge road at the side of his shop
at about 3.45 pm on July 9 a woman came
along and shouted out to him. He identified
that woman as the prisoner. She shouted out
something to the effect that she wanted to get
to Tonbridge quickly.

Witness's father, who was present, talked it
over with him and they decided that, as they
were going part of the way to Tonbridge,
they would give her a lift. They drove her all
the way to Tonbridge.

Prisoner told witness during the journey
that she came from a town similar in name
to Bolton – he could not remember the exact
name. She said her children had been evacu-
ated to Cornwall, that her husband was in
the Air Force, and that her mother was very
ill. She wanted to get to Tonbridge to meet
some friends who were going to take her to
Tunbridge Wells.

Prisoner had a long parcel, wrapped in
brown paper, with her all the time.

Witness said they dropped her at St. Mary's
Road, Tonbridge, almost opposite the police
station, between 4 and 4.15 pm.

At the Old Bailey Mrs Ransom was
found guilty. She escaped the gallows
but was declared insane and sent to
Broadmoor.

William Smith moved to Paddock
Wood, and went on to improve on his
humble beginnings, becoming an Army
sergeant and, in civilian life, a highly
skilled engineer. He died in 2004.

Capel Country Friends

Mike Temple

One of the great tests of humanity within a community is the way it cares for its older residents. In this modern world where people enjoy a longer life span, it is frequently accompanied by loneliness following the death of a partner or physical disability. In our parish, there was one person who became aware of the needs of the aged and was prepared to do something about it.

Capel Sports and Social Club provided an entertainment for Capel Country Friends for very many years. This was their 25th anniversary celebration at the Friends' Christmas lunch in Goldsmid Hall; Lady d'Avigdor-Goldsmid cutting the cake flanked by Pam Wenham and Albert Simmons. On the extreme right is Florrie Sceal.

Harry Veall was the farmer at Bank Farm in Tudeley, but he was also very active in many other community roles such as being a governor at Mascalls School in Paddock Wood, a JP and a long term churchwarden at the parish church of All Saints, Tudeley. In 1963, Harry became aware of the lack of any provision for the older members of the parish and decided that something had to be done on their behalf.

Being the proactive man that he was, he gathered a few friends together for a meeting that was thought to have been held at the old St Luke's church in Five Oak Green. Amongst those that attended were some well known names such as Albert Simmons, Brian Darbyshire, Jack Stonebridge, Ken Stinton, Micky Smith and Les Musthill. It was decided that the best way to get people together was to attract them with the prospect of a good meal, so a Christmas dinner was organised at the Goldsmid Hall. Of course, there was no finance available at that early stage, so they did their best to exploit the generosity of local people and businesses, particularly the pubs that donated a variety of drinks for the occasion. Charlie Simmons provided the turkey.

It was a great success. Harry Veall was voted in as Chairman with Albert Simmons as Vice Chairman and the rest of the initial group formed the committee. It was also decided that the name of the group should be 'Capel Country Friends'. A pattern of events soon emerged with the committee meeting on Wednesdays at the Men and Boys' Institute (later the Scout Hut) where events were organised such as regular 'charabanc' trips to the south coast, notably Eastbourne, where the Congress Theatre was regularly visited. Other popular destinations were Hastings, Drusillas Animal Park and The Royal Horticultural Society Gardens at Wisley.

Christmas lunch at the Goldsmid Hall sometime in the 1960s served by (standing left to right): Joan Simmons, Jean Humphrey, unidentified, Freda Simmons and Ken Stinton, whose job it was to serve the gravy. Seated centre-left is Harry Rose. Attempts to identify the other diners were not successful.

There is no doubt that it was the Christmas dinner that became the main annual event, one that tested the committee's talent to the full. As the cooking arrangements in the Goldsmid Hall at that time were inadequate, the meal was prepared at Capel School under the eagle eye of the then Headmaster, Ken Stinton. He arranged transport across to the hall not only of the meal, but also the school piano that was needed for the after-dinner entertainment. It was on these occasions that the early talents of members of the Sports & Social Club were displayed together with such memorable groups as the Banjo Band, regular visitors from Hawkenbury.

It is heartening to remember that those older folk who were too ill or disabled to attend were not forgotten. The Rev Frank Forbes was the vicar in those early days, and he, together with his wife, prepared Christmas food parcels that they delivered to their homes.

Capel Country Friends has now passed its fortieth year and still enjoys an active programme with Celia Worraker as the chairman. The Christmas dinners are still held, Charlie Simmons has continued to provide the turkeys and monthly meetings which used to be held in the Scout Hut now take place in Five Oak Green Village Hall. It is the continuity of groups such as this that provides such great value and strength to the social fabric of local communities.

The Alders

The Alders is often described by people from outside the area as a "blink and you'll miss it" sort of place, and it would indeed be more accurately described as a hamlet than a village. It is something of an enigma, for the signs at its approach announce the straggle of buildings as 'Capel', although long-term residents resolutely call it 'The Alders', insisting that 'Capel' is just the community around the church which long ago gave its name to the entire civil parish. Until recently the Post Office insisted that both were actually part of Five Oak Green. Compounding the confusion, the stretch of Alders Road from its junction with Sychem Lane to the Alders stream was formally not part of this parish at all, but in the parish of Pembury!

With the construction of rows of farm workers' cottages and other agricultural buildings in the middle of the nineteenth century, the opening of an ale house named 'The Alders Inn', and subsequently a combined shop and post office, a separate hamlet with its own identity was established. Although the shop has closed, the pub remains to give a heart to the community which even the Post Office now recognises as distinct from Five Oak Green.

The following two articles by Don Foreman, who lives in the hamlet, look more closely at the inn and the former shop and the contribution they made to the life of the parish in times past.

The Inn, the Old Stores and some of the cottages that make up The Alders photographed in 1976.

The Alders Inn

Don Foreman

The Alders Inn at the end of 1983

What is now The Dovecote Inn in Alders Road was, until the name was changed in 1987, The Alders Inn, and as that was its name for most of its existence that is how it is referred to throughout this article.

Quite how long an ale house has stood on the site has yet to be established, some suggest almost 300 years. Jim Perks, who was landlord in the mid-1980s, even puts a date on it (1712), unfortunately such antiquity is entirely legendary. The Pembury Tithe Map of 1843 shows no buildings at all along this part of Alders Road save for the old cottage whose site is now occupied by the modern bungalow Springfield. In confirmation, the architectural style suggests that both the present pub and the cottages either side of it were built in the middle of the 19th century.

During the time about which this article is written, the pub was owned by E&H Kelsey, who operated the Culverden Brewery in Royal Tunbridge Wells. Kelsey was later taken over by Green, which soon after was bought by Flowers, which in turn became part of the Whitbread Group. Subsequently Whitbread itself ceased to be an independent brewery and The Alders Inn was a free house for more than 20 years until, in 2006, it was sold to Enterprise Inns plc. and once again became a tenancy.

Bert and Vera Allcorn became tenants in 1953. They took over from Ernie Hastie, a former prison warder, and he was preceded by Alf Roberts. Before him the landlord was William Adams, while records show that in 1909 Ernest Ford was behind the bar. Their first day was

28th August, which by coincidence was also the first day of that year's hop-picking season. Guessing that the Allcorns would not be prepared for the prodigious thirst for which hop-pickers were renowned the brewers did not wait for their first order but supplied 400 crates of light ale and 400 crates of brown ale – all of which had gone in three days!

In the early days of Bert Allcorn's tenancy beer was 8d (the equivalent of 3 pence) a pint, and the usual lunchtime

Huts at Church Farm in which the hop-pickers from London used to stay. They were but a short walk from the inn.

takings were £7-£8. But, as they had soon discovered, during hop-picking it was a different story.

Every autumn up to 500 hop-pickers (including their families) moved onto the nearby Amhurst Bank and Church Farms alone, and it must have been difficult to cope with the surge of eager customers at opening time. At least during the Allcorn's time the drink was served in glasses and bottles. Jim Harman, now living in Croydon, worked on Mr Thirkell's farm as a boy during the 1940s when, as an evacuee, he stayed with relatives at Rose Cottages in Half Moon Lane. It was hard work, but he especially enjoyed being with the shire horses and liked to go with the men to The Alders Inn, where, he

recalls, beer used to be served by filling customers' mugs from a pail.

During the two hours of one autumn lunchtime session in 1955 takings reached a record £100, which means the equivalent of almost 3,000 pints had been sold! Not all of this was in the form of pints, of course, but included many crates of beer which were taken away to the hoppers' huts and caravans to keep them lubricated until evening opening. Nevertheless, Bert and Vera's son, John Allcorn, remembers it took five hours to wash and dry the glasses afterwards.

In their early days as landlords the Allcorns charged hoppers a deposit of one shilling (5 pence) on every glass, which was in excess of the cost of the beer they contained and a considerable sum in those days. This was in order to discourage theft and careless (or even deliberate!) breakage, but this was found to adversely affect sales and so was dropped after a couple of years.

Alders Road would be lined by parked vehicles, and drinkers spilled outside the pub making the road almost impassable. John Robbins parked his jellied eel stall at the front of the pub and did a roaring trade providing a good old London speciality to the pickers. The pub itself was packed to the doors, even though its chairs had been removed (partly to make more room and partly because otherwise they would have been broken or stolen). All that was left were simple benches around the walls and a few old tables. One of the benches, still in the pub and now beautifully upholstered, came from a station waiting room. There was a piano, of course, and plenty of people willing to hammer out a tune for the hoppers to sing and dance to.

Many of the hop-pickers were London

dockers on holiday, and they brought with them goods which, in the days before container shipping, they had been able to 'acquire' during the course of their work. The landlord was offered all sorts of things.

Even though Bert also had a full-time job in London as an inspector for a weighing machine company, usually the Allcorn family were able to run the pub themselves, but at busy times casual bar staff were engaged from the locality. Their one regular member of staff was the cleaner, Kate Bellingham, who lived in No.3 Alders Cottages. She had her own way of doing things, and would not use a new-fangled vacuum cleaner. Nor would she accept Mrs Allcorn's invitation to join her for a cup of tea in the sitting room; she thought that as a 'servant', that was not right!

The pub sold mainly beer and spirits. There was little demand for wine, which was specially ordered for the few more sophisticated customers, most of them passing trade. Mild served straight from the barrel was the most popular drink, but during the winter a pin (a cask holding four and a half gallons) of strong old ale called Stingo was available.

Very little food was sold in pubs then, and The Alders was no different from the rest, offering just hot pies, sandwiches, bags of plain crisps containing salt in a twist of blue paper, and the usual pub delicacies such as pickled eggs.

Those were the days of traditional pub pastimes, with card games, especially

One of the darts teams that played against The Alders Inn was The Queen's Head in Five Oak Green. The Queen's Head team is pictured here in the mid-1950s after winning a local league cup. Standing (left to right): George Gullivan, Reg Jenner, John Brockman, Bill Twort, Ted Wigmore, George Rowe and George (Spud) Simmons. Seated: Dennis Simmons, the Mayor of Tunbridge Wells, Albert Brockman with the cup, the Mayoress, and Horace Vousden.

cribbage, being the most popular, but there were also dominoes, shove ha'penny and darts. The Alders had its own darts team, playing against others from the pubs in Five Oak Green and nearby villages.

What is now the dining area was a brick floored room with a low ceiling, which was not removed to reveal the rafters until some years later. It was used as a store room for most of the year and opened up in August and September to provide extra public space for hop-pickers. Their room being lit by paraffin lamps which smoked and smelled, former hoppers still affectionately remember the pub as 'Paraffin Jack's'. When the introduction of mechanisation in the late 1960s brought about a dramatic decrease in the number of hop-pickers, the room was converted into a saloon bar. It was at this time that the

pub's clientele began to change: with greater car ownership more customers drove out from Tonbridge and Tunbridge Wells. Until then at least three-quarters of the regular customers lived within walking distance, and most of them were agricultural workers.

Two of the regulars, Bert Towner and Bill Humphrey, were well-known village characters. Bert worked at Badsell Park Farm and later for Mr Bridges at Brook Farm. He was short, with a round ruddy face and walrus moustache, and lived in a 'tumble down' old house on the site of the bungalow 'Springfield'. Except for three weeks each autumn when he was drying hops he went to the pub every lunchtime and evening without fail. Frank Thirkell and James Buggs remember him as a skilled hedger and very good with live-

Bert and Vera Allcorn with their son John sharing a last drink before taking their leave of The Alders.

stock. Bill, also short but well-built, was a wagoner who looked after the Buggs' farm horses, and lived in Sychem Lane.

There was a children's room where the pub cellar is now, a bare and cheerless space furnished with only benches and a table. No attempt was made, or expected, to provide anything to keep the youngsters entertained while their parents enjoyed themselves in the bar.

The public bar, to the right of the front entrance, was floored in brown lino. Its interior walls were not exposed brick as they are now, but were plastered and wall papered.

The toilets were built against the wall of the house next door, now separated from the pub by the drive to its car park. For women there was only one toilet, albeit with a double seat, but when necessary a female hop-picker would be stationed at the door of the gents' while her friends used the gully inside!

The provision of enough toilets was a perennial problem throughout the parish during hop-picking. David Fry said that on Lydd Farm pits were dug, lined with lime, and then corrugated iron sheds erected over them. Some pickers, unfortunately, did not always trouble to use the facilities provided, and Brian Turner recalls that it was advisable to tread warily when walking field edges in the autumn! Domestic arrangements were not much better, the six families living in Alders Cottages sharing three communal privies.

Behind the pub Bert and Vera Allcorn kept pigs, guinea fowl, turkeys, chickens, geese and ducks, carrying on the old country tradition of families achieving as great a degree of self-sufficiency as their land allowed.

The Allcorns retired from pub life in 1974, as The Courier reported in its issue of March 15th:

RETIREMENT MEANS MOVE TO OTHER SIDE OF THE BAR

RETIREMENT for Mr Herbert Allcorn, landlord of The Alders pub in Five Oak Green means a move to the other side of the bar. This week he and his wife moved out – to their new home three doors away at 7 The Alders Cottages.

However, this retirement does not mean that Mr Allcorn is giving up work. For the last 21 years, while he has been licensee at The Alders, he has also continued full-time working as a weighing machine engineer in London. This year he will have completed 50 years' service with the company, Henry Pooley Ltd.

How he managed to combine two full-time jobs is no mystery to his customers. "The wife has practically run the place single handed" he said. In the evenings he and his married son, John, who works for a Tonbridge printers, lend a hand.

For five days before they moved out the pub was the scene of a continuous round of parties. On Monday night Mrs Allcorn stood behind the bar for the last time. "I still enjoy the social side of pub life but couldn't keep up with the work. I am sorry to go – we have made so many friends. But we shall still be seeing them on the other side of the bar."

Mr Allcorn feels that a publican inevitably becomes a "father confessor." "In my time I have helped make out wills and fill in divorce and income tax papers for my customers," he said. "This is a nostalgic moment for me, even if I am only moving down the road."

He remembers fondly the early years behind the bar. "Hop-picking was a big thing in those days," he said. "In our first week here we sold 300 flagons and more than 700 dozen pints of beer."

Now, more than thirty years after Mr and Mrs Allcorn retired, the inn continues to attract customers at a time when modern pressures and changes in lifestyle have forced others in neighbouring parishes and across the country to close.

Indeed the Alders Inn, too, closed for a time in the 1970s.

As increased mobility killed off village shops, so it provided opportunities for many village pubs with enterprising landlords. As a free house The Alders has been improved by successive owners. Improvements started with the new toilet extension added by Jim Perks in 1984, and the complete re fitting of the bar area by his successor Graham Vamplew. Later, the space which had once been the store and hop-pickers' room was designated a dining area, and with a great improvement in the choice and quality of meals offered the one-time agricultural labourers' ale house has been transformed into a pub restaurant attracting customers from a wide area.

The Alders today showing the changes that have been made to what is now the Dovecote Inn.

The Alders Stores

Don Foreman

There must be many people who drive along Alders Road who notice the unusual bow window on the house next to the pub, the bright red post box next to its front door and, if they are very observant, the brackets on the wall at first floor level.

If they are *exceptionally* observant they might even have spotted the deep scratches on bricks around the door frame. They may have wondered whether the house once had another purpose, and they would be right, for this was once the little hamlet's very own general store and post office.

The bow window displayed shop goods, the post box (still in use) was for customers to post their letters, the brackets supported a large sign advertising 'The Alders Stores', and those mysterious scratches were where generations of delivery boys had sharpened their slate pencils.

Invaluable information about the old shop has been supplied by Mrs Lynne Assirati:

"When my family moved into the property in April 1984 we were told it is at least 200 years old, but we have not seen any proof. Two years later we were visited by the Playfoots, by then an elderly couple, who had the shop in the early 1930s and ran it for over 20 years. They were adamant that it dated back to 1650, but could offer no evidence to support the claim.

The Alders Stores around 1960 when it was owned by Mr Lundie Rees and provided a useful service for the small hamlet, especially at hop-picking time.

At the end of the 1960s the stores had been converted to a private house which retains the shop window and the post box.

"What is obvious is that the property consists of two small cottages 'two up, two down', which were at some time knocked together, presumably to convert the building into commercial premises with living accommodation. This is supported by the fact that there is evidence of a staircase, now gone, leading up from the room which was once the shop, suggesting that the cottages were not purpose-built commercial premises. At what point this became the village store, bakery and post office, and how the business expanded, we do not know, but the shop's bow window is Victorian, and the 'VR' on the post box indicates that it received its Post Office licence before 1901. The previous owners told us that they believed the bakehouse and granary were 170 years old, but we now know that the absence of any buildings on the 1843 tithe map proves they were mistaken.

"Our visitors told us they had moved in with six children. There was no indoor toilet or bathroom, and the kitchen was a very small room with cooking done on a huge Victorian range. They built on a new kitchen, in which a bath was also installed (it was not uncommon to have baths in kitchens in those days) but still had to go outside to the WC. Water was heated in a copper and poured into the bath, and on bath night Pa Playfoot would be first in. After he had finished his place was taken by each child in turn, and Ma was last. By removing the cooking range and knocking down the former kitchen wall they created a larger living room behind the shop area.

"Except for the pub and its grounds they owned all the buildings and land immediately adjacent, renting the corner cottage to a couple who helped in the shop and to look after the livestock. The Playfoots kept prize-winning pigs (the piggeries still exist) and cured their own bacon. They also kept hundreds of chickens on the upper floor of what is now Orchard Cottage."

Mrs Assirati's visitors were not the first Playfoots to run the Stores. They said the business had been in the family for more than 100 years, and Kelly's Directory names Thomas Playfoot as the owner in 1895. It was certainly in the family for several generations.

During its heyday The Alders Stores was extremely busy. Every evening at hop-picking time the little shop was full, and in order to satisfy demand extra stock was held – even the living room was stacked with supplies from floor to ceiling.

But the huge, and welcome, influx of customers was not without its problems. To prevent pilfering chicken wire mounted on wooden frames was fixed over both shelves and counter, leaving an opening just large enough for goods, once paid for, to be handed over.

Edgar Playfoot, grandson of the owners during the middle years of the last century, remembers there was a series of storerooms at the side of the shop (now

Orchard Cottage); one was for dry goods, another for meat, with sides of pork and lamb hanging from hooks, and another for paraffin etc.

As well as custom in the shop, there was a long delivery round taking goods to outlying farms and private houses and to workers in the fields and hoppers' camps. Edgar Playfoot said that the horse and cart was superseded by a Ford 'Model T' van, which was later replaced by a Morris van. During hopping provisions were delivered to the camps at 6 a.m., so it was an early start.

The Playfoots sold the business as a going concern around 1957 to Mr William Lundie Rees. He was succeeded in the early 1960s by the somewhat eccentric Mr & Mrs Tippen, who in turn sold it to Mr & Mrs Orr. Business stead-ily declined, and by the summer of 1969 the need for a general store in such a small community had gone. Even the post office offered only basic postal services, pensions and the like being dealt with in Five Oak Green. When Desmond and Jean Orr hung the 'closed' notice on the door for the last time they had already begun the process of converting The Alders Stores into a private residence. Sadly, Desmond Orr, who was much older than his wife and had been in poor health for some time, died in what had been the shop's living room. It was as a private house that the new owners, Mr & Mrs O'Neill, bought it.

The story of pubs and shops in hamlets like this has been the same throughout the country. Rural businesses depended on a relatively large (families with 10 children were not unknown) and static local

Mr Charles and Mrs Rhoda (nee Simmons) Martin with six of their children pictured in 1907. They all lived at what is now 5, The Alders, next to the Inn. Then it was a two-up and two-down cottage with an outside privy typical of the hamlet. Their seventh child, Stanley, was born there the following year. All seven went to Capel Schools.

population, and in places like Capel this was augmented by an inflow of seasonal workers picking cherries and soft fruit in summer, hops in early autumn and then apples and pears in late autumn. This extra custom over several months, especially September hop-picking, must have helped sustain The Alders Inn and Stores for the rest of the year.

During the 1960s the move to mechanised picking, and to a lesser extent the increase in imports causing orchards and soft fruit fields to be lost, meant that business in the pub and shop dropped away markedly. Combined with this, greater car ownership and the opening of supermarkets enabled residents to travel to nearby towns to buy a wider range of groceries, and more cheaply, too.

The Alders Ghosts

There are two residents of The Alders who were not available to share their reminiscences. They are the ghosts seen in the block of buildings formed by the pub and former shop.

Among those who have reported seeing an old lady wearing a bonnet are previous owners of the old shop, and she is believed to have been seen wandering through the building and its outhouses by others more reticent to speak of their brush with the supernatural.

The pub is the scene of even more ghostly happenings: electrical appliances have broken down without any fault being found; water has dripped from the ceiling from a non-existent pipe; a securely fixed shelf inexplicably fell off a wall but the glasses stored on it mysteriously remained unbroken as they hit the floor; strange noises have been heard, and one publican's dobermann dog on several occasions barked at something invisible to its owner and refused to go upstairs.

The most extraordinary experience so far recorded was that in the 1980s of Tracey Perks, daughter of Jim, the landlord. She saw a figure of a man in an upstairs room, let out a 'silent scream', and ran down to the bar to relate what had happened. When she had composed herself and described the man he was identified by long-time regulars as Alf Roberts, who had died there in around 1946, almost 40 years earlier.

If you order spirits in the pub, be careful you don't get more than you bargained for!

Goldsmid Hall: 110 years of history

Gill Hoare

In 1895 the local Kent newspapers were full of articles on the Agricultural Depression and the plight of the rural unemployed. However, in the Tudeley area Sir Julian Goldsmid, owner of Somerhill House and Estate, was providing employment for his workers by building a Hall. The building was designed in the Arts and Crafts style so fashionable at the time and was constructed with local materials – timber from the estate, bricks from Castle Hill brickyard and locally-made nails. One of the present villagers, Mrs Lillian Luck, remembers her father, Ernest Catt, telling her how he helped to dig the footings when he was just a teenager.

Sir Julian Goldsmid came from a wealthy merchant and banking family and was a well respected MP and philanthropist. Sadly he died in January 1896 and his obituary in the 'Kent and Sussex Courier' reveals that the Hall was not complete at the time. As Sir Julian left eight daughters and the estate was entailed to the male line, it passed to a young cousin, Osmond d'Avigdor. Later that same year, Osmond took the additional name and arms of Goldsmid by Royal Licence.

Early Days

In April 1897 Goldsmid Hall was officially opened by Mr A.G. Boscawen, the local MP, and that August employees from Somerhill House and estate were invited to attend a ball there to celebrate the marriage of Miss Estelle d'Avigdor (sister of Osmond) and Mr George Nathan (one of Osmond's university friends). It may have been this event that inspired Estelle and George Nathan to paint a mural for the Hall two years later. The painting was executed on paper, probably with paints made on the estate, and mounted on a backing of hopsacks before being slotted into an arched relief at the far end of the Hall. The mural shows a pastoral scene set only yards from the Hall near Park Farm (then called Home Farm) and it depicts various villagers of the time. These are believed to be Bill Shoebridge (pointing), Charlie Fowler (the young boy), Mr Flint and Mr Stert.

At the Hall's first anniversary in April 1898, Mr Osmond d'Avigdor Goldsmid reported that during the first year total attendances had numbered 1,236, with 62 members of the Working Men's Club and 18 members of the library. A regular Sunday School was held at the Hall and there had been two dances as well as lectures and concerts during that year. Mr Boscawen revealed in his speech that the Hall was built as a 'Working Men's Club for the neighbourhood, where they could all meet as friends for recreation and amusement and mutual improvement, putting aside all political and religious differences.' In spite of the ban on political topics, Mr Boscawen then proceeded

Sir Julian Goldsmid

to give a lengthy talk on the importance of Free Trade with China and Japan!

In the early years a number of concerts and plays were held at the Hall, mainly to raise funds for the Parish Sick Relief Fund. Osmond d'Avigdor-Goldsmid, his sisters and his brother-in-law, George Nathan, all took an active part in these events by acting in comedies and playing short piano pieces in concerts. Villagers and other locals also displayed their talents by playing instrumental pieces, singing ballads and reciting both dramatic and comic poems. A certain Dr Pollen's

'inimitable recitations' and 'amusing anecdotes' seemed particularly popular and usually earned 'a vociferous encore'.

When the Hall was first built it had a high stage at the mural end of the room. Under this there were stairs running down to a cellar room where a billiard table was kept. A boiler was also located in a separate cellar at the opposite end of the Hall and this heated the water that ran through pipes to warm the property. Lighting was by gas and vestiges of the original brackets can still be seen just inside the entrance. A house was built adjacent to the Hall for the use of the caretaker. However, one of the downstairs rooms in this house held the library, which contained a range of books including romances, adventure stories and biographies of famous explorers. Inside each book was the instruction, 'No book shall be lent to anyone in whose house there is an infectious illness'.

Between the Wars

Villagers remember attending children's parties at the Hall in the 1920s and 1930s and also taking part in the annual Capel school play. The children painted the scenery themselves and it was often quite ambitious and spectacular. During performances, curtains were hung around the stage to form two wings, one at each side. There was a fireplace in the right-hand wing and the ladies or girls were given the privilege of changing in this warmer side. The Goldsmid family attended most of these events.

In the 1930s the Hall was the venue for a very active youth group where young people could play billiards, darts and have sing-songs. Dancing was particularly popular. Lil Luck can remember attending dances when she was very young. However, her mother always went with her and during the dancing, the mothers would sit and chat over a cup of tea. Some of the younger boys also accompanied their sisters on the walk to the Hall and would sit with the caretaker, Mr Stanford, on the stage watching the dancing. Gradually the younger girls and boys learnt to dance by copying the older ones. They had to rely on an adult to play the piano for them, but at the adult dances there would be a proper band situated on the stage.

The Tudeley Scouts started life at Goldsmid Hall and, only a year or so later, there was great excitement when they won the County Competition at the Whitsun Camp held on land behind the Hall.

The Goldsmid family continued to take an interest in the Hall. In December 1933 it was the venue for a party to celebrate the coming of age of Second-Lieutenant Jack d'Avigdor-Goldsmid (Osmond's younger son). Employees of the Goldsmid family were invited to the event, which consisted of a dinner with speeches followed by a 'ventriloquial entertainment' and dancing.

Osmond d'Avigdor-Goldsmid (who was created a baronet in 1934) died in 1940 and the estate passed to his elder son, Henry.

Post Second World War

During the Second World War evacuee children poured into the area so that the local school at Capel and the schools in Tonbridge were filled to bursting. Goldsmid Hall was therefore taken over and used as extra classrooms, as well as serving as a drill hall in the evenings for the Home Guard. Gordon Sceal, the youngest member of this Home Guard unit, remembers that they had no official instruction manual and were taught by veterans of the First World War. The Hall was also used for many fundrais-

ing events during the war – in particular dances to raise money to buy new Spitfire aircraft.

During the Forties the caretaker's house was split into two separate flats for the use of workers from the Somerhill estate. In the post-war years the Hall fell into a bad state of repair though it was still used for the occasional social event. It was also (and still is) a Polling Station for local and national elections and a designated disaster relief centre. For many years it was also used as a church during the hop-picking season. Gordon Sceal and his wife, Florrie held their wedding reception here in 1949. The place was in such a bad state that it took them three days to clean it before the event!

The 1960s to the Millennium

After the Second World War, the Parochial Church Council had taken over the Hall management and by the 1960s a few groups were beginning to use the Hall again. Sir Henry d'Avigdor Goldsmith, therefore, suggested that a group of Hall users should get together to form a Management Committee. He also offered to provide some labour and materials to help renovate the Hall. So the village set too, cleared the garden, cleaned and painted the Hall and new heating was installed. The ground floor of the house was also converted into a meeting room, with a kitchen, an extra toilet and storage space. In 1966 the new Management Committee appointed Gordon Sceal as caretaker.

Since then, the building has been used by a number of organisations such as the Capel Country Friends, Capel Sports and Social Club, Capel Gardeners' Society and the various badminton clubs. But above all the villagers have used it to mark milestones in their lives with wedding receptions, christenings, children's parties, birthdays and anniversary celebrations. Some very memorable parties have taken place here over the past forty years including one to mark the Queen's Silver Jubilee in 1977.

In the early 1970s the stage was removed as it restricted the play of the badminton groups. As in the early days of the century, concerts once more became part of Tudeley social life so a temporary stage would be erected when needed. Villagers remember the lead singer from the Tunbridge Wells Amateur Dramatic Society performing at the Hall each year and a banjo group, all in their 80s, who came on stage in their carpet slippers. One of the highlights of the year, however, was the Capel Sports and Social Club's Annual Concert, which relied solely on local talent.

Originally there had been no need for a car park at the Hall, as most users lived locally. However, by the 1960s many people from outside Tudeley were attending events at the Hall so car parking had become a serious problem. Eventually Sir Henry donated a piece of the orchard on the opposite side of the drive to the Hall, and a car park was built there.

In the early 1990s the owners, the Hadlow Estate, asked for a more economic rent for the Hall. As the Management Committee felt that it could not raise the increased amount from the letting income, Lady d'Avigdor-Goldsmid arranged a respite period while all options were considered. However, after her death in June 1997 no solution had been reached and so, consequently, late in 1999 the property was advertised 'to let' on the commercial market.

'Saving' the Hall

A public meeting was called at the Hall in March 2000 and was attended by about

Lady d'Avigdor-Goldsmid

150 villagers. The overwhelming feeling was that the Hall should be saved for the use of the local community and so a steering committee, comprising both old and new villagers, was set up. This committee conducted an initial survey of facilities and the recreational needs of the local population. It became obvious that the full repairing rental suggested by the owners could not be met from the letting income from the Hall, so it was decided to negotiate for a 99-year lease. In addition, the accommodation fell far short of current standards, though the physical state of the property was sound. Funds therefore had to be raised for the purchase of the lease, for the renovation of the Hall and for the building of an extension to meet health and safety and disabled access legislation. As a first step the Goldsmid Hall Trust was set up in April 2001.

By the following summer the necessary funds had been raised from Kent County

Council, Tunbridge Wells Borough Council, the Community Fund (Lottery), Wren (Waste Management Company) and other bodies as well as local fund-raising events held at the Hall. By June 2002 the Trust started negotiating the lease (for the Hall without the house) with the owners and by the following April this lease was signed.

The Rolf Harris Window

The signing of the lease coincided with a programme the BBC was making on Marc Chagall in the series 'Rolf on Art'. In March 2003 Rolf Harris visited Tudeley Church to see the Chagall windows and to do preliminary sketches for a stained glass window in the Chagall style. He designed it in two panels: the left hand one was in dark blue to depict night time and contained an image of Tudeley Church, the right hand panel had

a gold background depicting daytime and contained images of a Kent oasthouse and an ass (which to Chagall was a symbol of happiness). The design also included other images such as angels and doves echoing those in the Chagall windows in the church.

The BBC was keen that this window should be placed in Tudeley village and the Goldsmid Hall seemed to be the ideal location. The window, completed by Rolf together with Judy and Keith Hill, two Kentish glassmakers, was installed on 30th May 2003. A wine and cheese party was organised for that evening and Rolf Harris agreed to attend. So on one of the hottest May evenings in living memory, Goldsmid Hall (packed with partying villagers) achieved national fame by being filmed as part of the 'Rolf on Art' programme. Then, after having been

Although one or two members of the hall trust were not able to be present most of them appear here photographed with Rolf Harris in the centre. They are, left to right: Teresa Curtis, John Spoor, Vicky Cheesman, Natalie Booker, Rolf, June Spoor, Ron Hoare (chairman), Val Coleshill and Keith Bromhead.

installed for only a few hours, the window was taken out again and put into storage as building work on the new extension was about to start.

New Beginnings

The architect, Roger Molyneux, had designed the new extension to complement the existing building. It runs the full length of the Hall, two of the existing windows having been enlarged to form two access doors (one of them incorporating the 'Rolf Harris' window above the door). The new facilities include a modern, fully-equipped kitchen, a sunny meeting room, male, female and disabled toilets as well as storage cupboards and new disabled access. Building work was completed on 31 December 2003 and the formal opening ceremony took place on 4 March 2004 with Archie Norman, the MP for Tunbridge Wells, opening the refur-

bished and extended Hall for the use of the local community.

In 2005 the Goldsmid Hall Trust was able to raise the additional funds to pay for the re-roofing of the property. Then consideration was given to the deteriorating condition of the mural. A survey was carried out in the parish, and it appeared that most local people wished to retain the painting, or at least a copy of it. Advice from experts revealed that the cost of restoration would be more than £20,000 and it was felt that such expenditure could not be justified. The decision was therefore made to return the original mural to the descendants of the Goldsmid family and commission an updated version as a replacement. In January 2007 Cecile Boswell-Brown, a Tonbridge artist, started work on the new mural. Over the next two months villagers and other users of

Some of the visitors who went to the hall for the first viewing of Cecile Boswell-Brown's new mural. The photograph illustrates the way the two former windows were changed to provide access to the new extension. Rolf Harris's new window in the style of Marc Chagall is seen above the door on the left.

Mary Bromhead, Lillian Luck and Val Coleshill serving refreshments, provided free by 'THE TUDELEY OAK',
at the open morning when villagers were able to see for the first time the new version of the mural.

the hall watched with interest as the new painting emerged. It is not an exact replica of the original but the same pastoral scene has been retained, interpreted in a modern, vibrant style. The new mural was unveiled to villagers, Hall users and the local press at an open day on the 3rd March 2007.

Another milestone in the history of the hall was reached on the 30th November 2006 when Gordon and Florrie Sceal retired after 40 years of caring for the property. During that time they had, as a team, worked as caretaker, cleaner, booking secretary and treasurer. As a gesture of appreciation for all their work and dedication the Goldsmid Hall Trust

decided to name the meeting room 'The Sceal Room'.

The hall is now being used by a number of local groups during the week on a regular basis and at weekends it is heavily booked for wedding receptions, children's parties and other family celebrations. Fund-raising activities continue in the form of Bingo sessions, occasional quiz nights, barn dances and other events.

By April 2007 the Goldsmid Hall had provided a valuable local community centre for 110 years. With its updated and enhanced facilities it is set to continue serving the village for many years to come.

Gordon and Florrie Sceal outside 'their' room.

Glossary

Advowson: The right of presentation to a church benefice.

Bloom: a mass of iron hammered or rolled into a thick bar for further working.

Bloomery: a forge or mill producing blooms of wrought iron.

Chafery: part of the forge where the pig iron was further refined.

Fallow deer: a deer with branched antlers, typically having a white spotted reddish brown coat in summer.

Finery: a hearth where pig iron was converted into wrought iron.

Glebe: Land belonging to a church.

Hundred: An ancient division of an English county, originally supposed to contain a hundred families.

In Capite: Held immediately of the Crown.

League: An old measure of length, usually estimated at about three miles.

Lowy: A little used description of an area of territory extending about a league from a town. Tonbridge was one of very few towns in England to have a lowy.

Nodules: small rounded shape of rock as in a large pebble.

Pig iron: the first stage of refining iron ore which when molten was poured into sand moulds forming 'sows'.

Porchester: a settlement of Roman origin near present-day Portsmouth.

Tabular masses: rock laid down in flat, plate form.

Tithe: A tenth of a farm's agricultural income collected for the support of the clergy.

Palaeontology: Study of early Ice Age Quarternary Period – geological term for most of the Ice Age from 1.6 million years ago.

Sources and acknowledgements

This account of the history of some aspects of Capel Parish would not have been possible without the considerable help, advice and memories of parishioners past and present, of various organisations and institutions and access to both specialist and more general publications.

Many of the sources used will be apparent in the context of the individual articles; those that may not are set out here.

The Parish

Tonbridge School Historical Society Study, 1964; Tricker, Roy, Guide to St Thomas a Becket Church; Neervort-Moore, Mary, Guide to All Saints Church; Patrick Sheard, Kent Libraries staff at Tonbridge and Royal Tonbridge Wells.

Bagshaw's Directory

James Buggs, James Simpson, Stuart Lyons (The George and Dragon), Tonbridge Poll Books, and Burke's Peerage and Baronetage.

Capel School

Capel School logbooks, Capel School Admission Registers, extracts from managers' minutes, Census returns 1851, Ordnance Survey Maps 1869 and 1809, answers to Centenary Questionnaires, recollections of former pupils, and personal memories of Mr and Mrs C. K. Stinton.

The Ice Age

The Natural History Museum, Kent and Sussex Courier, Jan 31st 1986, On the Track of the Ice Age Mammals, A. J. Sutcliffe, published by the British Museum ISBN 0-565-00869-2, Mrs M. Stinton's personal recollections and notes.

Hospitals

Thanks are due to Mrs Mary Stinton for permission to use material from her publication the Little Hoppers' Hospital and to Mr Frank Chapman for material from his Nostalgia column in the Kent and Sussex Courier.

The Postern

Published sources: Cazlet F. (1994) Historical study of the Postern Estate, Tonbridge; Chalklin C. (1960) A Kentish Wealden Parish 1550-1570 (Thesis for Bachelor of Letters, Oxford); Chalklin C. 1994 Georgian Tonbridge, Tonbridge Historical Society; Chalklin C. (2004) Iron Manufacture in Tonbridge Parish with special reference to Barden Furnace,c.1552-1771, Archaeologia Cantiana

Vol. CXXIV, 2004; Chapman F. (1976) Book of Tonbridge, Barracuda Books; Cleere H and Crossley D. (1985), The Iron Industry of the Weald, Leicester; Department of Environment List of Buildings of Special Architectural or Historic Interest; Pevenser N. (1976) West Kent and the Weald in 'Buildings of England'; Straker E. (1931) Wealden Iron, David and Charles; Victoria History of the Counties of England, History of Kent Vol. 3 (1932) Ed. By William Page, St Catherine Press and Wooldridge S. and Goldring F. (1962) The Weald, New Naturalist, Collins. The author is particularly grateful to Dr C. Chalklin for his suggestions for reference material on the Wealden iron industry and for permission to draw on his thesis "A Kentish Wealden Parish 1550-1750". Helpful suggestions also came from Mrs Sheila Broomfield, secretary of Tonbridge Historical Society.

Charcoal Burning

Albert Simmons, Charlie Simmons, Gordon Sceal, Barbara Smith, Jean Cox and Pam Jones.

The Alders

The author wishes to acknowledge the help and information he received from Frank Thirkell, Shirley and Brian Turner, Diane Collins, Marjorie Parks, Josie and Peter Knight, John Allcorn, Jim Harman, Edgar Playfoot, Lynne and Robert Asirati, David Fry, Jim Perks, Jane May, Henry Acott, Ray Large, Reg Jenner, Shelley Page (The Dovecote Inn) and Josie Harrison (The Queen's Head).

Goldsmid Hall

The author wishes to thank Mrs Chloe Teacher for granting access to the press cuttings books of Mr Osmond d'Avigdor-Goldsmid and to Mr Gordon Sceal for conducting most of the interviews required for this article. Valuable information came from Mick Moon, Gordon and Florrie Sceal, Albert Simmons, Tom and Don Large, Lillian Luck, John Cavey and Doreen Cogger. Other sources included: Debrett's Peerage and Baronetage, obituaries of Sir Julian Goldsmid in Tonbridge Free Press and Kent and Sussex Courier (10th January 1896), article on the agricultural depression in the Kent and Sussex Courier 14th August 1897), extract from account of the first anniversary of Goldsmid Hall in Tonbridge Free Press (9th April 1898) and the BBC programme Rolf on Art in the style of Chagall.

The Society would like to record its gratitude to Paul Chalklin for his commitment, advice and skill in making possible the publication of Capel Explored and also to Peter Tulloch for the similarly generous gift of his time and skill in repairing and restoring old photographs and taking all the recent ones. It also wishes to thank Graham Whibley for collating and placing on CD the society's extensive photographic archive

Subscribers

Lisa Elizabeth Jones
B.S.Wise
Doris Large
Stephen Large
Gerry & Marion West
Pam Whibley
Graham Whibley
Marjorie King
Graeme & Sue Connell
Mrs Grace Baldock
Richard & Claire Songhurst
Mrs Pam Mabb
Gwendoline Lamb
C.M.S. & Lynn Robinson
Joanna Robinson
John Robinson
The Rev Dr Jeremy and
    Rev Pamela Ive
Diana & Mick Allchorne
Frances & Peter Hawken
L.E.Mair
Mr D. Gregory
Mrs M.A.Gregory
V.F.Thorp
Mr & Mrs R.E.Taylor
Brian Cubbon
Chris & Jose Twynam
Mick & Janet Sells
Christine Langridge
Bea Foreman
Pat Figgett
Christine Cockcroft (Coatsworth)
David Coatsworth
Pat Aldridge
G.R.Sceal
Mike Temple
Denise Low (nèe Phipps)
Bryan Phipps
Edna M.Meanwell

Mr & Mrs D.Vincent
Bob Anthony
Paul & Phyllis Card
Mrs J. Hughes
Bryan and Jane More
Martin & Fiona Pengelley
G.E.J.Wood
Ian & Dawn Davis
Neil & Katharine Jones
Pam Jones
Andrew Stanley
Pam Stanley
Jon Fryd & Diane Skiello
Don Foreman
Capel Primary School
Dennis Ingram
Maurice & Laura Simmons
Pamela B.Wickens
Mr John G.Ellis
Nick & Hilary Andrews
Jean Cox & Brian Martin
Norman & Susan Pickett
Mr R.A.Large
Jean Knight
Mrs Jackie Root
Julie Underwood
Maureen A.Tulloch
John Rumens
Ben Watson & Emily Hildred
The Stinton Family
Mike & Michelle Perry
Sharon Saunders
Lynne Weekes
Clive & Margaret Andrews
Brian & Shirley Taylor
Philip French
Tony Mignacca
Ron & Gill Hoare
Helen Marke

Jason Brumpton & Clare Wooldridge
Tony and Pauline Carter
Mr & Mrs B Verey
Mr Frederick & Mrs Diane Collins
  (nèe Blanche)
Mrs Sue Bryant
Mrs Anne-Marie Richards (nèe
  Collins)
Audrey Anstey
Harold Acott
David Passey
Sharon Burgess
Carol & Charles Mackonochie
Isobel Lucy Elizabeth Wright
Oliver Christopher William Wright
John E.Vigar
John Bridges
Capel Grange Residential Home
Roger and Daphne Dolding
M & G Thompson
Mr S. Potterton & Dr K. Potterton
Marie Smith
John & Brenda Jones
Sadie Ann Youngs
Frank Edward Sands
Geoff & Lilias Newby
Megan Forster
Dora Delves
Mrs James Teacher
Martin and Gill Stagg
The Strawson Family
Don and Maureen Lynch
The Vanns Family
Mr & Mrs J.P.Williams
Mr M.T.Hills
Audrey Jenner (nèe Passey)
The Summers Family
Ann & Bryan Smith
James & Elizabeth Edwards

Jonathan & Catherine Howlett (nèe
  Edwards)
Ashley & Jessica Warren (nèe
  Edwards)
Mrs June Darbyshire
Paulette & Patrick Sheard
Mrs L.Inhester
Mrs Margaret Lawrence
Ivan Hughes
Ian & Angela Pattenden
Mrs June Lepper (nèe Phipps)
Mr V. Greenstreet
Mrs Hosmer
Bill & Melanie Harrington
Ted & Joan Vanns
Miss J.M.Debney
The Greenwood Family
John Arthur Coomber
Jean and David King
Ms Sarah Cobell
Maureen Jane Worsell
Daphne Males
Mr S.Mead
Mrs Jennifer May Crowley
Alison Williams
John & Jennifer Naylor
Keith & Mary Bromhead
Peter A.T.King
Mrs Wendy Robb
Mrs Margaret Smith
Mrs M. Cole
Nick Stevens
Gillian Langstaff (Founder &
  Matron, Capel Grange Residential
  Home 1980-2005)
Mrs M. Ellis
Mrs D.E.Jones
F.M.Thirkell
Mr J.Perks

Index